PINK HERRINGS

PINK HERRINGS
Fantasy, Object Choice, and Sexuation

Damien W. Riggs

KARNAC

First published in 2016 by
Karnac Books Ltd
118 Finchley Road
London NW3 5HT

British Library Cataloguing in Publication Data

A C.I.P. for this book is available from the British Library

ISBN-13: 978-1-78220-174-8

Typeset by V Publishing Solutions Pvt Ltd., Chennai, India

Printed in Great Britain

www.karnacbooks.com

Dedicated to my parents

$$\dfrac{FM}{\overline{\exists x\ \overline{\Phi x}}}\quad\dfrac{MF}{\exists x\ \overline{\Phi x}}$$

Sharon Robert

CONTENTS

ACKNOWLEDGEMENTS

I begin by acknowledging the sovereignty of the Kaurna people, the First Nations people upon whose land I live and work.

Thanks are due to my classmates and teachers at the Australian Centre for Psychoanalysis, where some of the initial thoughts that led to this book were developed. Special thanks to Julie-Anne Smith, Esther Faye, Leonardo Rodriguez, and Ursula Paton for your words of encouragement, and to the organising committee of the 2012 International Lacan seminar at which Dr. Colette Soler spoke, which was an inspiration for this book.

I owe a considerable debt to my friends who have listened to me talk about this book, and in so doing have helped me to work through my own thoughts about it. Specific thanks go to Louise Messenger, Tom Gross, Stephen Hicks, Amy Patterson, Kate Foord, Alison Ravenscroft, Jess Hondow, and Sophie de Rohan for your insights and support.

It is also important to thank Ian Parker, who believed in this project from our very first correspondence about it, Patricia Gherovici, who inspired me with her own book and who so kindly agreed to write an endorsement for this book, and Chloe Elizabeth, who created the amazing artwork that appears on the cover of this book.

Finally, thanks must go to my children, Gary, Jayden, Liam and Damian, who put up with me spending so many weekends reading and who always remind me of why I do the work I do.

ABOUT THE AUTHOR

Damien W. Riggs is an Associate Professor in social work at Flinders University and an Australian Research Council Future Fellow. He is the author of over 150 publications in the fields of gender/sexuality studies and mental health. He also works in private practice as a Lacanian psychotherapist.

This book takes a key concept from the "later Lacan"—sexuation—and shows that it is crucial to the way we approach sexual difference and gender in Lacanian psychoanalysis; both in the way we track our way back through Lacan's own work, back to the founding texts of that tradition, and in implications for the way we handle transference in the clinic. As a reading, an innovative re-reading of Lacan through the lens of sexuation, the book already accomplishes something seemingly impossible; it shows the reader in a clear accessible way how to make sense of sexuation as a distinctive concept in the Lacanian tradition, as an alternative not only to "sexual difference" and "gender" but also to contemporary debates which aim to "queer" psychoanalysis.

And there is more, for the body of the book is dear to Lacanians and indeed to all psychoanalysts of whatever persuasion, of whatever theoretical or sexual orientation, that is, Freud's own work. A close reading of Freud's case studies rediscovers, as all "returns" to Freud have attempted to do, the staging of later psychoanalytic concepts elaborated after his death but which now bring his writing alive again. Damien Riggs shows how sexuation is at the heart of Freud's exploration of fantasy and object choice. This is where the clinical implications of this reading take shape in an argument that takes forward not only our understanding of Freud's own clinical practice but our own. We begin to see that the infant's puzzle about the "choice" made by those who are their first objects will set the coordinates for their own choice, about what they will come to speak about as their own "gender" and their own "sexuality".

Psychoanalytic clinical and theoretical work circulates through multiple intersecting antagonistic symbolic universes. This series opens connections between different cultural sites in which Lacanian work has developed in distinctive ways, in forms of work that question the idea that there could be single correct reading and application. The Lines of the Symbolic series provides a reflexive reworking of psychoanalysis that transmits Lacanian writing from around the world, steering a course between the temptations of a metalanguage and imaginary reduction, between the claim to provide a god's eye view of psychoanalysis and the idea that psychoanalysis must everywhere be the same. And the elaboration of psychoanalysis in the symbolic here grounds its theory and practice in the history and politics of the work in a variety of interventions that touch the real.

Ian Parker

INTRODUCTION

This book began with a title—*Pink Herrings*. At the time I was reading Patricia Gherovici's wonderful book *Please Select Your Gender* (2010), in which she suggests that "the phallus is less a red herring" (as Tim Dean, 2000, suggests it to be), and more a "read" herring. Like gender, Gherovici suggests, the phallus is "subject to interpretation, and it will always be read like a text" (p. 231). This pun struck a chord with me, and led me to think about how the idea of the "read herring" might be put to work analytically in the service of ideas that I was grappling with at the time.

In the same year that I read *Please Select Your Gender*, I was studying at the Australian Centre for Psychoanalysis as part of my formation as an analyst. As would be expected in such a course, we read widely from the works of Freud and Lacan. When it came to reading Freud's (1909d) case study of Paul Lorenz—the Rat Man—I was struck by the fact that throughout the case (and in Lacan's later reading of the case) a range of different terms are used to describe the site of the rat torture that constitutes Lorenz's obsession. Admittedly I was reading Strachey's English translation of Freud's writing, but what stood out to me was that in places the site of the torture were the buttocks, in other places the anus.

In Miller's (1979) translation of Lacan's account of the torture in "The neurotic's individual myth", the word "rectum" is used.

These differing words used by Freud and Lacan seemed to me to allude to different implications of the torture. If the site of the torture were the buttocks, then the rats would chew their way through the person's body, from back to front. If the site of the torture was more specifically the anus or rectum, then the torture was about the rat entering the person's body as a means of escape. Of course it is far too simple to treat these two modes of torture as mutually exclusive, as I came to see in my own analysis, in which the rat torture became something of a theme.

When I was a child my family and I visited a local tourist destination, where a collection of wax models were displayed in varying states of medieval torture. One of these models was being subjected to the very rat torture described by Lorenz. As a young child I interpreted what I saw as the rats trying to escape the burning coals by chewing their way through the buttocks: from front to back. Arguably this interpretation spoke of growing up in a family where female genitalia were referred to as a "front bottom" (distinguished from the anus which was referred to as a back bottom). In this sense, and as I suggested above, the binaries of back and front, inside and outside, were perhaps less distinguishable than might at first appear to be, as Lacan's account of the Mobius strip so cleverly demonstrates.

Perhaps another reason why I was struck by the differing terms utilised by Lacan and Freud in discussing the case of Paul Lorenz related to my identification as a gay man. One of the questions that arose as part of my analysis was "why am I gay?" Perhaps more specifically, my question was "what subjective position does being gay allow for me in relation to men and women?" Amongst gay men the words "buttocks", "anus" and "rectum" operate in complex and shifting ways, not necessarily in ways that are entirely distinct from those discussed by Lorenz in terms of his obsessions about the rat torture. Most well known in this regard is Leo Bersani's (2009) account of anal intercourse in his: *Is the Rectum a Grave?* In this book Bersani discusses how receptive anal intercourse is culturally seen as demeaning to men who engage in it. Such men are often referred to as "passive" (as opposed to "active") sexual partners, and the negative cultural value attached to passivity is seen as undermining the masculinity of men who are receptive partners.

In the face of this negative cultural value accorded to passivity, Bersani suggests that if the receptive rectum is indeed "a grave in which the masculine ideal [...] of proud subjectivity is buried, then it should be celebrated for its very potential for death" (p. 29). Whilst Bersani's wider critique of the stigmatisation attached to passivity in general and receptive anal intercourse more specifically warrants ongoing attention, I would nonetheless suggest that there is a considerable gap between the "should" of Bersani's statement and the reality of how gay men who are primarily or exclusively receptive partners are viewed, both in society at large, and within gay communities. Bersani's celebration of the death of a masculine ideal sits uneasily alongside the social death that can be the price paid by men who are viewed as passive receptive partners.

These arguments about receptive anal intercourse and the death of a social ideal can be tentatively mapped onto Freud's case. With regard to Lorenz, if the rat in the rat torture is indeed a tool of penetration (of the anus or rectum, as Freud and Lacan respectively refer to it), then the rat brings with it the possibility of death in a literal sense, but it also acts as a potential agent of death in terms of masculinity. Whilst Bersani suggests that this is something to be celebrated, the question that arises for me is whether the rat torture as narrated by Lorenz (and ventriloquised by Freud) is indeed something to be celebrated, or whether it is something to be feared (or indeed perhaps it is both). My point here is not that Bersani is suggesting the actual implementation of the rat torture, but rather that metaphorically the question that he raises is whether the reading of the rat torture by Freud *as a bad thing* is the only, or even best, interpretation of its meaning to Lorenz.

To return to the title of this book, then, my thoughts about the multiple meanings of the rat torture in the case of Lorenz, alongside my reading of the work of Gherovici (2010), initially coalesced into a question about whether or not there are moments in Freud's cases where certain possible readings of (homo)sexuality are elided, and conversely, possible moments when more is made of homosexual identifications than was warranted. Through its connections to the use of the pink triangle in Nazi Germany to signify men who were homosexual (and the later resignification of the pink triangle as a symbol of gay culture), a pink herring by this understanding is thus a mode of reading for homosexuality within a text.

Having developed the idea of writing a book titled "Pink Herrings" that would explore possible misreadings in Freud's most well-known cases, I first sought to identify whether the term "pink herring" had been used in this particular way before. The first instance of the term I found appeared in a journal article published in 2002, in which Morris suggests that J. Edgar Hoover engaged in a rhetorical tactic referred to as a pink herring. This tactic, Morris suggests, involved Hoover perpetuating a moral panic about homosexuality in order to ensure that publically he was seen as a heterosexual man. This account of a pink herring is certainly of a kind to that which I elaborated above, though it is different in the sense that it emphasises a pretence of heterosexuality utilised to mask a "true" homosexuality.

The second example of a pink herring that I found used in academic writing involved a more simplistic substitution of the word "red" for "pink", without the accompanying development of an actual theory of what a pink herring is. In a journal article published in 2005, for example, Larcano engages with one argument that has been made against gay marriage, namely that it will lead to the legalisation of other kinds of purportedly "undesirable" marriages (such as polygamy). Larcano refers to this claim as a pink herring, referencing the association between pink (possibly the pink triangle mentioned above) and homosexuality.

In an initial attempt at further unpacking what my own use of the term pink herring might mean, I wrote the following:

As with so many aspects of Freudian psychoanalysis, misunderstandings abound. Perhaps one of the most frequent misunderstandings relates to whether or not Freud may be read as advocating for a pathologising view of homosexuality, or whether he adopted a more supportive stance. The former reading has resulted in academic writings that have either engaged in exegeses of Freud's work aimed at finding support for a pathologising understanding of homosexuality (i.e., an anti-gay approach), or writing that has refuted Freud's work under the assumption that it is homophobic (i.e., an anti-Freud approach). For those who have viewed Freud's work as affirming of homosexuality, there has been an equally problematic recouping of his work. In its most obvious form this appears in writing that emphasises the needs of "gay patients" or the "gay aspects" of an individual's unconscious. Whilst such accounts are intended to be affirming of such patients (and indeed their "gay analysts"), what they do is attribute both gender and sexual orientation to the unconscious, which represents a fundamental misreading of Freudian psychoanalysis.

This paragraph indicates what has become something of a marginal understanding of the term pink herring in regards to the overall message of this book. Certainly there is some ground to be gained by considering how homosexuality is understood across a range of psychoanalytic approaches. At the same time, however, I would argue that in many ways such a focus is itself a pink herring, given the fact that identifying the "causes" of homosexuality and thus advocating for analytic approaches that either engender understanding or attempt to "cure" it are ultimately reductive misunderstandings of Freud's theories. In other words, writings that locate themselves under the banner of psychoanalysis are perhaps a long way removed from psychoanalytic praxis as outlined by both Freud and Lacan when they take as a serious clinical issue the need to account for homosexuality as a unique entity in terms of etiology.

Having said that, it is important to state that my approach in this book is not intended to dismiss texts that have sought to counter the appropriation of psychoanalysis when used in the name of homophobia. Nor is my approach one that is dismissive of texts that have sought to examine the history of psychoanalysis as a meaning-making enterprise, and how it has potentially been misunderstood in terms of its stance on homosexuality. Further still, my approach is not one that denies the specificity of the experiences of gay or lesbian analysands, nor is it one that denies the specificity of the experiences of gay or lesbian analysts, particularly those who practice in contexts that they experience as homophobic. And finally, my approach is not dismissive of cultural and literary theory that has utilised psychoanalysis as a framework through which to understand the world around us, specifically with regard to (homo)sexuality.

Different to any of these approaches, however, in this book my use of the term pink herrings is intended to maintain a clinical focus on sexuation that can account for the experiences of lesbians and gay men (amongst other groups), without focusing *per se* on homosexuality. This might seem counter intuitive, and certainly in this introductory chapter I will not be able to do justice to the argument that I make in this book, reliant as it is upon Lacan's complex and extensive writings on the topic of sexuation (in addition to those who have more latterly taken up this topic). What can be said briefly here, however, is that a pink herring, as I now understand the term to mean, does indeed refer to instances where imputations are made about the sexual orientation of Freud's analysands, but the "answer" to these imputations is not to assert a more "correct" reading of their sexual orientation. Rather, following Lacan, my interest is to consider the fantasies at play in six of Freud's cases, to consider how these fantasies position both his analysands and those to whom they are closely related in particular ways (as can be seen via a focus on the analysands' object *a*), and what this can tell us about their sexuation as masculine or feminine.

A pink herring, then, has at least two meanings in this book. The first, and more obvious one, was the position I took when I first conceived of this book. In this instance a pink herring refers to a misreading, and thus is closely aligned with Gherovici's (2010) notion of the "read herring". In the case of homosexuality—which is not *per se* Gherovici's focus—this notion of the pink herring is most definitely useful, but it is only a starting place in terms of reading Freud's cases. The second understanding of a pink herring, and one that is the central focus of this book, is how a focus on sexual orientation (as it is commonly used in contemporary social scientific research) adds very little to our understanding of the unconscious in terms of its operations. This is not to naively suggest that the world at large—and more specifically the homophobic world at large—bears no relationship to what an analysand speaks about when on the couch. Rather, it is to suggest that an analysand's position in terms of sexuation is about the "choice" they make in terms of their relationship to knowledge and jouissance, a choice that occurs well before any conscious awareness of social norms as they circulate in the world around them.

Some points about language and concepts

Whilst it is impossible to prevent oneself from being misread, it nonetheless seems important to offer up some further introductory comments to the reader, specifically for the reader who may not be overly familiar with Lacanian psychoanalysis. In the following chapter I outline in detail my understanding of Lacan's account of sexuation, so that will be the place to go if you seek clarity on that topic and my approach to it in general. What I offer here are instead caveats about the limits of the claims made in this book, and some specificity about their application in regards to terminology.

Some readers may already have gotten to this page, and seen words such as "choice" and "clinical focus" used in association with homosexuality. Indeed, anyone who has read the preceding pages could not help but have noticed the repeated use of the word "homosexual" itself. For many, the word homosexual will seem hopelessly dated, if not offensive. For some readers it may seem to naively accept the heterosexual/homosexual binary, for others it may be read as reducing sexuality to behaviours and practices rather than identities, and for yet others it may be exclusionary of a range of sexual identifications (such as bisexuality, pansexuality, asexuality, and so forth).

Likewise, the word "choice" may irk some readers, who see the language of choice used by those who oppose the rights of lesbians and gay men, dismissing such rights as undeserved on the basis that, in their estimation, homosexuality is a choice. To speak of sexuation as a choice, as I did just three paragraphs earlier, may thus be incendiary for some readers. It may seem to presuppose a book that is dismissive of the lives of gay men and lesbians, or one that is aligned with those who deny the rights of lesbians and gay men.

Finally, the clinical focus of this book—both through its examination of clinical cases, and its discussion of clinical implications in the final chapter—may seem to serve only to reinforce the notion that homosexuality should primarily be understood within the domain of the clinical. Indeed, I alluded to that in reference to my own analysis in suggesting that one of my key questions—at least on the surface—was "why am I gay?" As someone who in their other academic work is highly critical of normativity within lesbian and gay communities, I am familiar with the accusation that I must be suffering from "internalised homophobia"— that I am a self-hating gay man who critiques other gay men from a place of non-acceptance.

The astute reader can perhaps guess at what my response to any of these accusations will be: that they are all pink herrings in the first sense I outlined above. All of these pre-emptive accusations I have ventriloquised on behalf of the reader focus on but one way of understanding sexuality. What they focus on are conscious understandings of sexuality: how we align ourselves politically, the words that we preference as the best descriptions of our experiences, and the modes of discrimination against which many of us feel we must speak. I hope that I am clearly on the public record about my position on all of these matters, and that the curious or concerned reader can follow up my work elsewhere.

The difference in this book—as signalled by the second definition of pink herrings provided earlier—is to shift the focus away from binary categories, to take a step away from etiological accounts of identity, and to instead engage with what we don't know about ourselves, namely our unconscious. An identification, in the everyday use of the word, is something that is conscious—it is something that we know we are doing, and which we have a certain degree of control over. The operations of the unconscious are of an entirely different register. The operations of the unconscious pertain to that which we don't know we are doing, where our choices are shaped by our entry into language.

This then begs the question of my use of the word choice above. The choice in terms of sexuation, following Lacan, is not really a choice at all. When we are born we are, in essence, biological beings. There is a small list of things we need to exist as such: primarily food and water. But when we are born it is not particularly easy for us to ask for these things. All an infant can do, or at least what infants do that is perceived as a cue for food and water (and all that comes from them, namely waste), is cry. The response to that cry is of course highly differentiated by the caregiver, and hence each of our experiences of being cared for (and perceiving what constitutes care) is highly differentiated.

To become a person beyond being a biological being, Lacan suggests, requires language. This does not necessarily mean speech—my students often ask me whether psychoanalysis is inherently ableist if it privileges spoken language. Yes, spoken language is privileged within psychoanalysis (and in most of the world around us), but language more properly refers in this first instance to the back and forth that typically occurs between a caregiver and an infant. An infant makes a demand for something they need (food or water and their by-products) and the caregiver responds to this in some form. At first, Lacan suggests, the demand and response are perceived as one and the same thing. The caregiver is omnipotent, so the infant thinks, or perhaps more accurately, the caregiver and the infant are perceived as one and the same thing. This perception of oneness is a central concept within Lacanian thought, as we will see throughout this book.

There comes a point, however, at which the infant perceives themselves as a separate entity to the caregiver. In his early work, Lacan referred to this as the mirror stage, referencing the period of an infant's life where they look in a mirror and comprehend that it is themselves they see in the reflection. Over the course of his work, however, Lacan shifted away from this type of developmental account, and instead saw the mirror stage as one that produces dissociation, rather than association. In Lacan's early account the infant associates themselves with the image. In Lacan's later accounts, the infant experiences a dissociation between the "whole" image of themselves they see in the mirror, and the sense they have of their body as both "whole" only in relation to a perceived oneness with their caregiver, and not whole in the sense of any unified experience of the physical and psychical demands that come from differing parts of their body.

This dissociation, particularly with regard to the perception of wholeness or oneness with the caregiver, is profoundly disturbing. In an attempt at dealing with this sense of dissociation, the infant (or perhaps more correctly by this stage, toddler) latches onto particular parts of the caregiver that are seen as representative of them. This may be a smell, a look, a taste, a body part, a sensation. Any of these can serve as reminders of a much sought after sense of oneness with the caregiver. Of course at this time, when the child is engaged in processes of meaning making, they are engaged in language. And it is this "cut" into language of which we have little choice. Lacan, following Freud, does of course elaborate what happens if this cut into language does not occur, namely psychosis. So certainly it is not true that everyone becomes what Lacan terms a "speakingbeing"—someone who has undergone the cut into language. Nonetheless, it is the case that most human beings do enter into language, though of course how they do so is highly differentiated.

As I noted above, the perception of oneness that an infant has is a central concept in Lacanian thought. Lacan argues that once we become speakingbeings, we come to believe that we can communicate both our needs and wants to another and they will in turn respond in some fashion. Yet by default of the fact that we have entered into language, we are in effect alienated from any sense of oneness with our caregivers. Instead, this sense of oneness was an illusion of our life prior to language, and we cannot return to the other side of the cut into language. What we do instead is hold onto the pieces of our caregiver that we believe symbolise that sense of oneness. These are what Lacan referred to as object *a*. These are signifiers of something that we have retrospectively attributed meaning to, but which existed, we believe, prior to our entry into language—our entry into signification.

Perhaps the clearest way that Lacan describes this process of signification is in terms of the fictional story of Robinson Crusoe. Specifically, Lacan refers to footprints left in the sand by Friday, the man befriended by Crusoe. Lacan suggests that the footprints themselves are a sign, they are something concrete in the world, though with no inherent meaning, and importantly that they are not Friday himself—they are already one step removed from him. In the case of the infant and caregiver, one sign might be a certain caress, or a certain roughness whilst feeding. These are concrete phenomenon in the world similar to the footprint, in that they don't carry an inherent meaning, and they are not the caregiver themselves.

Lacan then speaks of Crusoe effacing the footprints, wiping them away. All that is left is a trace of them, perhaps a disturbance in the sand. This trace isn't the footprint itself, it isn't a sign. In the case of the infant and caregiver, the trace might be a feeling that accompanies a certain caress roughness whilst feeding. It isn't the actual phenomenon of a caress or roughness, though there is a trace of that in it. Finally, Lacan speaks of the signifier. If Crusoe wants to remember where a footprint was, he might put a marker there—a cross for example. This cross comes to signify the trace of the footprint. So it isn't a foot, nor a footprint, nor even over the passage of time will it be the trace (given the disturbance in the sand will be washed or blown away). All it is is a marker—a reference. In the case of the infant and caregiver, the signifier is much harder to describe than simply a cross. It could be anything that the infant comes to retrospectively associate with the trace. As I noted above, this ability to leave a marker is only possible once a child has entered into language, at which point all they are doing is leaving markers of something they can no longer reach. This reaching, Lacan suggests, circulates in a fantasy that allows the child to believe that they once had access to the person that the sign represents: it functions to deny the fact that they were never at one with the caregiver in the first place.

It is of course vital to clarify here how Lacan understood the relationship between the signifier and the signified (in the description above, the sign is what is being signified). In his seminar on Anxiety Lacan described the relationship between the two as such:

> The signifier, so I told you at one turn in the path, is a trace, but an effaced trace. The signifier, so I told you at another such turn is distinguished from the sign by the fact that the sign is what represents something for someone, whereas the signifier is what represents a subject for another signifier. (2014, p. 62)

This definition is centrally important to the argument that I develop in the following chapter, and the chapters that follow it. The sign (the footprint, the certain caress or roughness) represents something for someone—it is not another person to whom someone has immediate access. But even the sign is something to which we do not have access. What we have—what we are—is signifiers: signifiers in the unconscious, and as they constitute the language of the unconscious, are markers of a trace of a sign that represents something about someone to whom we have no access in the form of a oneness, and indeed to whom we never had the access we might wish we did. Importantly, this is true both for us, and for the caregiver with whom we seek that sense of oneness. So we are each a set of signifiers that represent our unconscious to another who is similarly a set of signifiers: when we speak to another, when we attempt to relate to or connect with another, we are one set of unconscious signifiers attempting to communicate with another set of unconscious signifiers. As I will explore further in the following chapter, there is thus an unbridgeable gap between any two speakingbeings, and it is how we attempt to bridge that gap (or feign that there is no gap) that is the focus of this book.

Of course some readers might find this account of the infants entrance into language entirely too negative. Nonetheless, it is a relatively accurate (if very brief) outline of a Lacanian account of how an infant moves from being a biological being to being a speaking being. Any sense of negativity, I would suggest, is however tempered by the fact of the choice I outlined above. The choice, for want of a better word, is to either stay in the illusion of a harmonious oneness with the caregiver (and thus experience psychosis), or to enter into language. Once we have made that entrance, as all of Lacan's work gives testimony and as this book elaborates in a very specific way, what we are trying to do is make up for what we feel we have lost (but which we never had).

Having provided this very brief outline of why I use the word choice in terms of sexuation, it is perhaps also important here to comment on my use of the word "caregiver". Much has been made in critiques of Freudian and then Lacanian psychoanalysis of the use of both the word "mother" (instead of caregiver or parent) and the emphasis upon the role of the father. In chapter two I will go into this in more detail, but to briefly summarise: following the cut into language, the child not only holds onto the objects *a*—the little pieces of oneness or what Lacan terms "jouissance"—but the child also attempts to find ways to re-establish the lost sense of oneness in concrete ways. In order to try and "repair" the relationship, the child seeks to either have or be what they perceive their primary caregiver wants or lacks. For most people, an armistice of sorts is declared by force of a figure of authority—by the figure of authority saying that the child cannot have their primary caregiver, cannot be all of what their primary caregiver lacks. This is Lacan's reformulation of the Freudian concept of castration—castration in this sense is not literal but rather metaphorical. Castration in the Lacanian sense is first the cut into language—the demand to the speakingbeing to acknowledge that the sense of oneness with the mother was illusory—and then the "no" of the authority figure who in some way or another tells or shows the child that they cannot have their primary caregiver. As I explore in detail in the following chapter, this does not stop the child from making unconscious identifications, whose aim is to be what the primary caregiver is perceived as lacking or wanting.

Perhaps most important within any Lacanian account, then, is the fact that what I have described above denotes positions with language, and that these positions within language structure the unconscious like a language. Whilst my relatively simplistic outline above of a Lacanian account of the cut into language could make it seem as though these are all moments or experiences available consciously, it is important to emphasise that instead they are positions within the unconscious, snippets of which possibly become accessible through analysis. Importantly, the snippets of what becomes accessible are signifiers—what becomes accessible in analysis is never the effaced sign that would give us direct access to jouissance.

To return to my use of the word caregiver in this first chapter, I have used this term following an argument made by Swales (2012), who suggests that the "mother" and the "father" are markers of positions within language. She offers instead the language of the "first Other" (i.e., the first primary caregiver) and the "second Other" (i.e., the person whose "no" marks the castration of the speakingbeing in terms of not being that which the first Other is perceived as wanting or lacking). Throughout the course of this book I alternate between these terms, using caregiver primarily when describing an actual relationship between a parent and child, using "desire of the mother" and the "no" (or name, as Lacan alternately termed it) of the father when referring to structural positions within language with direct reference to Lacan's work, and in some other instances I utilise Swales' language of the first and second Other to encourage the reader to make a break from the gendered readings that can all to easily come with the language of "mother" and "father". This last point is vitally important, as we will see in the following and subsequent chapters, where some authors who have engaged with Freud's cases have slipped into equating men with masculinity and women with femininity, which is antithetical to Lacan's account of sexuation. Similarly, in terms of Lacan's account of sexuation itself, I will argue in the following chapter that despite its use of formal logic, there still appears to be something of an implicit assumption that a child's first other will always be a mother.

It is thus important to emphasise that the term caregiver comes with no expectation about a particular form of care. Similarly, the language of first Other and second Other comes with no expectation that this is a mother and father, or even two parents (or only two parents). Cases of children in orphanages provide examples where a relationship is developed with a therapist who comes to stand for a first Other (Lefort, 1994). And a second Other may take the form of any person, or even representative of a person, that places a prohibition on the child's attempts at being or having the desire of the first Other.

Finally, the term "homosexuality" warrants comment. This book is not the place for a debate about the problems associated with the term itself. At the same time, it would be too simple to state that I use the term "homosexual" because Freud or Lacan do. Without pre-empting much of what is to come in the following chapter, what I can say here is that the jarring or troubling aspects of the term homosexuality are useful precisely because they force the reader not to slip into substituting more common words such as "gay", "lesbian", "man", "woman" into the account of sexuation that I provide in the following chapter. The term homosexuality is useful precisely because, at least in my reading, it signals a structural location within a system of signifiers in which one only makes sense in relation to another. This is not to accept wholesale a binary understanding of homosexuality and heterosexuality, but rather to think about how unconscious identifications exceed what we think we know about ourselves and our psychological make-up, and instead that our unconscious identifications are about positions within structures of fantasy in which homosexual, heterosexual, man, woman bear no inherent relationship to physical bodies, and instead are the product of unconscious positionings.

Point of divergence

As I alluded to earlier, the approach that I take within this book in examining sexuation in Freud's case studies differs, I think, wholly from other approaches that have examined the topic of sexuality in the context of (primarily Freudian or post-Freudian) psychoanalysis. In this section I want to outline in a little more depth what these points of difference are. My intention in doing so is not to suggest that my approach is any better than any other approach, but rather to emphasise the differences, particularly so as to prepare the reader for the substantive outline of my approach that I provide in the next chapter.

There is a now substantial and important body of literature on the topic of homosexuality *in* psychoanalysis. As I noted earlier, in terms of my own approach, I would consider this literature a pink herring, in the sense that it adds homosexuality (and specifically lesbians and gay men) onto a list of potentially diverse clients we might expect to see in the clinic. Included in this literature would be Abelove (1993) and Roughton's (2002) excellent historical accounts of the relationship between psychoanalysis and homosexuality; Drescher (1998), Lewes' (1988), and the many voices in O'Connor and Ryan (1993), all of which account for both the misuse of psychoanalysis in the name of homophobia, and psychoanalytic etiologies of male and female homosexuality; and a range of clinical accounts of analyses undertaken with gay or lesbian analysands, and the work of gay or lesbian analysts (e.g., see chapters in Domenici & Lesser, 1995; Sherman, 2005).

As a very heterogeneous set of writings, these texts are, I would argue, organised by a number of key assumptions. First, they assume that psychoanalysis should have something to say about homosexuality (and that what it has had to say in the past has been wrong, and should be corrected). Second, they assume that psychoanalysis has something to offer lesbian or gay analysands specifically in regards to understanding their homosexuality. Finally, these texts assume a specificity to the experiences of lesbians and gay men that it is expected will be born out in analysis. My point in this book is not that any of these assumptions are wrong. Rather, my point is that my approach differs entirely to the approaches adopted in these books. It differs in the most obvious way being that the texts I mention above are all informed by Freudian, or American ego-psychology post-Freudian approaches, whilst my approach is informed by the work of Lacan and those who adopt a Lacanian approach. Whilst a Lacanian approach is of course also a Freudian approach (as Lacan himself repeatedly stated), the language and arguably remit of a Lacanian approach differs in terms of its aims and intentions.

There is a second set of texts from which this book diverges. This is constituted by texts that are framed alternately as "queer", "postmodern", and "deconstructionist" accounts of psychoanalysis and homosexuality. Perhaps the most well-known amongst these are Judith Butler's many engagements with the works of both Freud and Lacan (e.g., 1992; 2002), Teresa de Lauretis' account of lesbian desire (1994), Dean and Lane's (2001) excellent edited collection of queer accounts of psychoanalysis and homosexuality, Tim Dean's sole authored book *Beyond Sexuality* (2000), and Lynne Layton's (1999) postmodern account of clinical practice and its relationship to gender theory. These books, in varying ways, seek to challenge and examine the truth claims made in the name of psychoanalysis, to deconstruct and reconstruct a psychoanalytic account of lesbian and gay desire, and to utilise psychoanalysis as a lens through which to read contemporary culture. Though all excellent, these texts differ from my own approach in that they primarily are not clinical in focus (Layton's work being an exception to this), and that to a certain degree their focus is on lesbian and gay identities and desires, which is different to my focus upon sexuation (though Soler's chapter in Dean and Lane's edited collection is an exception to this).

Finally, there is an important body of work that this book closely draws upon. These are books written primarily by Lacanian analysts, who work with Lacan's writings, and whose focus is upon sexuation. Key amongst these writers are Colette Soler (2000; 2006), Ellie Ragland (2000; 2001; 2004), Susanne Barnard (2002), Genevieve Morel (2000), Patricia Gherovici (2010), and Guy Le Gaufey (2005). These authors all engage with Lacan's formula of sexuation, which I will introduce in the following chapter. In this sense, my work does not greatly differ from their work in terms of the theoretical orientation. The point of difference comes in my approach to using the formulas of sexuation to develop an account that I then utilise in the identification of a particular set of pink herrings in Freud's cases, namely in his assumption of a correspondence between being assigned female and feminine sexuation, and being assigned male and male sexuation. Of course all of the authors I have just cited take as central this very critique of Freud, however their application of it in terms of theoretical focus is different to my own.

Conclusions

What this book aims to do, then, is develop a mode of reading sexuation, one that is, I hope, readable. There is much to be said for taking the time to read and re-read Lacan's large body of work. The complexity and nuance that his work offers is inspirational. At the same time, many of us have less and less time to read in such depth. My hope is that this book will make a contribution in a way similar to those cited above, a group of writers who have extensively engaged with and theorised from the work of Lacan, and whose works provides vital and much needed entry points into Lacanian psychoanalytic thought. By focusing on one specific aspects of Lacan's work—his later focus on sexuation—my intent is to provide a mode of reading psychoanalytic cases that can have direct application.

This is not to suggest that this book provides a "how to" guide for reading sexuation in the case of any analysand. The book itself it limited by the fact that it draws upon Freud's cases and the analytic material available in them. Nonetheless, what this book does do is provide an entry point to a way of thinking about sexuation and its application in the analytic setting.

Importantly, a focus on sexuation does not overwrite the need to focus on psychical structure (in terms of Lacan's account of hysteria, perversion, and psychosis), and indeed it is important to bear in mind that for each of the cases that I examine there was a diagnosis of structure provided by Freud. My suggestion, however, would be that given it would appear that a focus on sexuation can extend our analysis of cases where such a diagnosis is warranted, it may be even more useful in cases where a diagnosis is less easy to provide, but where a set of psychical coordinates may nonetheless help to orient the analysis. In the final chapter of this book, then, I provide an account of what a "clinic of sexuation" might look like, and how such a clinic would involve the work of mapping out the role of sexuation in the lives of analysands in ways that help us to understand the circulation of desire.

CHAPTER ONE

Lacan's formula of sexuation

A cross many of his seminars, Lacan spoke of the "sexual non-rapport" or the "sexual non-relationship". In the simplest sense, what Lacan meant by this is that after the infant as a biological being enters into language and becomes a speakingbeing—after they undergo the cut into language and then symbolic castration as enacted by the "no" of the father—they are denied access to the place where they perceived a sense of oneness with their caregiver. Intimate and caring relationships between people, Lacan suggests, are one way that we attempt to make up for this lack of access to what we perceive to have been a desired sense of oneness. Whilst certainly when we are physically intimate with another person we often engage with them through our bodies, Lacan suggested that what arouses our desire is something about the person that represents an object *a*. To put it bluntly, as Fink (1991, p. 77) does, a sexual partner is a "prop" or "medium" that supports our access to an object *a*. Our partner (or an aspect of them), then, in terms of our unconscious desire, is this object *a*, even if consciously we believe that our partner is the person we are being intimate with.

Sexual relationships are marked by a "non" in the unconscious, then, because the unconscious is structured by a series of signifiers that are already dissociated or at a distance from that which they stand for, as I outlined in the previous chapter. The kernel of the unconscious, to put it very simply, is not the fact of oneness with a caregiver, and it certainly isn't the caregiver themselves. Rather, at the kernel of the unconscious are signifiers through which we have retrospectively written a claim to a feeling of oneness with another. Whilst, through the work of analysis, we may decipher aspects of that language—the signifiers that for each of us tell the story of that sense of oneness—we can't cross back to a place before language where we can be in a fantasised place of oneness. The illusion of crossing back, we might suggest, is part of what drives us to engage in sexual or caring relations with other people, but as Lacan's account of the entry into language would suggest, once we have entered into language we are fundamentally cut off from that perceived place of oneness, and indeed it only becomes something that we perceive as "oneness" once we have entered into language.

In her work on Lacan's account of sexuation, Susanne Barnard (2002) suggests further that not only is the desire for oneness illusory, but even at the cellular level it was never a reality. Barnard elaborates on Lacan's (1998) analogy to the process of meiosis, which is the process of cell division involved in the production of a zygote. As Barnard notes, the zygote is not formed simply by the fusion of two gametes (sperm and egg), as goes the common sense understanding of reproduction. Rather, meiosis is the initial process by which half of the cells from one gamete join with half of the cells from the other gamete to form the zygote. The zygote that is produced is thus not a "one" produced by two. Instead, it is a one produced by a subtraction from two.

Barnard, following Lacan, makes the important point that this production of a one thus results in a remainder—a leftover that is not part of the one. To use this as a metaphor for a child, the one of the child as a speakingbeing is a partial product of at least two twos—the two of the gametes and the two of the infant/caregiver relationship. Whilst this might seem at first glance like two produce one, it is more correct to say that a one is produced through the impossibility of simply combining two wholes to make one: the combination is only partial. What is leftover, Barnard suggests—the excess—is what in the case of the child/ caregiver relationship becomes the object *a*. This excess is what fell to the wayside when the child entered into language and when the illusion of oneness was revealed to be simply that—an illusion. The object *a* are the little parts of excess that remain in the unconscious as reminders that there were two who for a period were experienced as one, even if they never were one.

Beyond the fact that at the cellular level one is not made up of two wholes (but rather parts), and beyond the fact that the unconscious of one person is not made up of two halves (but rather parts of the language of the caregiver and subsequently the language of the symbolic order—the "no" of the father), there is yet another way in which the "non" of the sexual relationship functions according to Lacan. In developing his account of the relationship between the signifier and the signified, Lacan utilised the example of the doors that are typically used to designate public bathrooms intended for men or women.

LADIES   **GENTLEMEN**

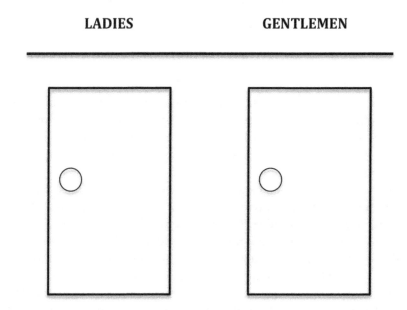

As Žižek (2002) notes, this depiction of the relationship between the words "ladies" and "gentlemen" (what are treated by Lacan as signifiers) and the doors (what are treated by Lacan as signifieds) tells us much about the sexual non-relationship. Typically this depiction of a relationship between the two signifiers is taken as indicating how children are instructed as to differences between people assigned male and people assigned female: the child needs to understand that there is a difference between these assignations in order to know which door to go through, and this difference is relative. Žižek, however, notes a second interpretation of the image of the doors. Whilst the signifiers "ladies" and "gentlemen" denote a difference, in terms of what is being signified there is no difference—the doors are identical. Sexual difference in this sense is not about differences in genitalia or chromosomes. Instead, it is about how we perceive ourselves in relation to our first Other. In this sense, there is no sign in the unconscious for the fact of sexual difference.

Žižek's (2002) point about there being no difference between the sexes at the level of the unconscious thus demonstrates again the "non" of the sexual relationship. Instead, what we have—as represented in the image above—are positions, a point I emphasised in the previous chapter. How Lacan elaborated these positions is the topic to which I now turn.

Lacan's formula of sexuation

It was in his seminar *Encore* that Lacan (1998) primarily developed his formula of sexuation. Based on his own version of formal logic, Lacan demonstrated that differences between speakingbeings in terms of sexuation are not the product of biological differences. Rather, he suggested, differences between speakingbeings in terms of sexuation are the product of our relationship to jouissance, the remainders of which appear as object *a*. Lacan suggested that there are two modes of jouissance: one that is typically referred to as masculine, and one that is typically referred to as feminine. These two terms, however, in many ways serve as a distraction, as the normative understanding of masculinity and femininity as binary categories can all too easily lead us to slip into understanding the two modes of jouissance as binary opposites associated with men and women. In order to understand why this is not the case in terms of Lacan's formula, it is important to unpack his formula in some detail. The following figure represents Lacan's formula of sexuation at its most familiar:

Masculine	*Feminine*
$\exists x\, \overline{\Phi x}$	$\overline{\exists x}\, \overline{\Phi x}$
$\forall x\, \Phi x$	$\overline{\forall x}\, \Phi x$

To understand this first representation of Lacan's formula of sexuation, the symbols continued within it require explanation. In formal logic, ∃ is an existential quantifier, and translates to "there is". In formal logic ∀ is a universal quantifier, and translates as "all". In Lacan's formula Φ is the phallic function: the operation of the cut into language that produces the speakingbeing and the castration that arises from the "no" of the father. In the formula Φ is thus a quantified function. Finally, in some of the quarters of the formula either the quantifiers or quantified function are negated. In formal logic, a negated universal quantifier— $\overline{\forall x}$ —takes on a quasi-existential meaning. Similarly, in formal logic a negated existential quantifier— $\overline{\exists x}$ —takes on a quasi-universal meaning. Finally, in Lacan's formula of sexuation the x stands for the speakingbeing.

With these explanations in mind, we can translate the formula as such:

Masculine	Feminine
There is at least one x which is not submitted to the phallic function	There is not one x which is not submitted to the phallic function
All x are submitted to the phallic function	Not all of an x is submitted to the phallic function

We can now unpack the formula a little further with reference to each side of the formula, starting with the masculine side. Whilst the two quarters in the masculine side are depicted as separate (and for the purposes of this book, as we shall see below, I will treat them as separate positions), they are nonetheless intertwined and hence must be understood as such. Starting with the bottom quarter on the masculine side, we have the statement that all x are submitted to the phallic function. This means that all speakingbeings who are located within this position have been subjected to the "no" of the father, which serves to restrict access to the desire of the mother (and thus limit phallic jouissance). This is true *for all* of those located in this position. This position, however, must be understood in relation to the position located in the top quarter of the masculine side, which states that there is at least one speakingbeing who is not subject to a "no" in terms of jouissance— one who has not had their phallic jouissance limited to only a particular group of people. This *exception* is the father of the primal horde as discussed by Freud in his *Totem and Taboo* (1937b). This is the figure who has unlimited access to phallic jouissance, and for whom there are no limitations (though importantly, this is not the position of psychosis, which is typically understood as the *failure* of the "no" of the father). With reference to Freud's figure of the father of the primal horde, then, this is someone who is not subjected to the prohibition on incest.

With the relationship between the two masculine positions in mind, Barnard (2002) tells us that the masculine side of the equation is a closed set with a fixed limit (the $\exists x \, \overline{\Phi x}$) that is external to the set whilst being a necessary part of it, and which thus produces the set as resting on the equivocation of the two quarters on the masculine side. As Barnard states:

> Thus while [the masculine speakingbeing located in the bottom quarter] is "whole" within the symbolic, the exception that delimits [them] precludes [them] from fully identifying with castration. One could say that while [the masculine speakingbeing located in the bottom quarter] is wholly subject "to", and hence "in", the symbolic, [they are] "in it with exception", that is, [they] "take exception" to it in some way. As a result, the fantasy of the subject not subjected to Law—the fantasy of no limit—determines masculine structure in an essential way. (Barnard, 2002, p. 177)

Turning to the feminine side of the formula, we are faced with a much more challenging task in attempting to explain its meaning. As I noted above, the two sides of the formula are not binary opposites, so it is not simply a matter of substituting the opposite meaning of the masculine side of the formula. Instead, and as Lacan discussed at length over many years, the masculine side of the formula denotes phallic jouissance, whilst the feminine side of the formula denotes an other jouissance. Importantly, however, this is not to say that those speakingbeings located on the side of the feminine are not subjected to the phallic function. The symbol of the x is used on both sides of the formula, noting that we are referring to speakingbeings, and hence those who are subject to the phallic function. Lacan's point, instead, is that those speakingbeings located on the feminine side of the formula are located in relation to the phallic function in an other way, and thus have access to an other jouissance (in addition to phallic jouissance, which ultimately is a failed jouissance as it is reliant upon a fantasy of being what the first Other desires, a fantasy that is never attainable, or indeed, following Lacan, 2014, cannot be attained for fear of destroying the object a that circulates within it).

Perhaps the most important way in which the feminine side of the formula differs from the masculine side is that it is not a closed set. We can see this in the fact that the feminine side does not include a universal exception. Instead, on the feminine side we have a negated existential quantifier—$\overline{\exists x}$—and we have a negated universal quantifier—$\overline{\forall x}$. In terms of the latter, instead of being a universal quantifier, we have what functions as a quasi-existential quantifier. Rather than the "all" of the masculine side written as $\forall x\, \Phi x$, we have a "not all". Importantly, this is not the same as the existential quantifier of the masculine side—the $\exists x$. On the masculine side the existential quantifier is an exception to the law. On the feminine side, the quasi-existential quantifier $\overline{\forall x}$ only indicates that "not-all" of the speakingbeing located in the bottom quarter of the feminine side is submitted to the phallic function. Of course this "not-all" sits in a relationship to the universal $\overline{\exists x\, \Phi x}$: there is not one x which is not submitted to the phallic function. How do we reconcile these two positions?

Guy Le Gaufey (2005) suggests that these two positions are reconciled by the fact that the feminine side of the formula is not a closed set, but rather it engenders a logic of the infinite. As Le Gaufey states:

> With these two contradictory writings, conjoined in the same deixis, Lacan posits a domain of individuals escaping any collectivisation that would produce an essence of them, as well as the definite article which, in French, is the sign of it. Hence the famous "The woman does not exist", a provocative residual statement from this search for the missing universal speakingbeing. [on the feminine side]

In the context of this book, I am reticent to continually restate the phrase "The woman does not exist"—written by Lacan as "The Woman"—as it can too easily make it seem as though it is women in the sense of people assigned female at birth who are located on the side of the feminine, and who do not exist. Nonetheless, it is important to understand that the side of the feminine is not constituted by an existential exception, and thus the feminine is not a closed set that would produce an essence. In other words, the feminine side of the equation exists—and thus there are speakingbeings located on this side of the equation—but on this side there is no claim to collectivity that would enable us to label the form of jouissance that is produced on this side of the formula. In this sense, the feminine side of the equation is conditional.

This further understanding of the feminine side of the equation as conditional enables us to unpack a little further the somewhat elusive meanings of the formulas for this side. Remember, the masculine side of the equation is a finite set bounded by one (or at least one) who is an exception, an exception who constitutes the rule for those who are located on the masculine side. On the feminine side there is no such position that sets such a limit. Instead, we have an open set, a set that is both entirely within the phallic function (we are speaking about speakingbeings here after all), whilst holding the potential for an other jouissance that exceeds phallic jouissance.

The clearest of the two positions on the feminine side of the formula to understand is: $\overline{\forall x}\ \Phi x$. Following Le Gaufey (2006), we can suggest that this position is one in which *not all* of the feminine subject in this position is subject to the phallic function. So this is a speakingbeing who perhaps exceeds the phallic function in some specific way, and who thus has access to some form of jouissance beyond the phallic. Importantly, this is not to say that the phallic function does not operate—if this were the case we would be speaking about psychosis and thus we would not be within the realms of the formula of sexuation. Instead, we are talking about a speakingbeing who might have accepted the phallic function in a very specific way, one that indicates there is something more to jouissance than that regulated by the phallus.

The other position on the feminine side of the formula—$\overline{\exists x}\ \overline{\Phi x}$—however, is something else again. This position is somewhat akin structurally to the position of the $\forall x\ \Phi x$ on the masculine side of the formula, whilst being entirely different to it. The $\forall x\ \Phi x$ is the speakingbeing, all of which is fully within the phallic function, but who accepts this position on the premise that there is an exception ($\exists x\ \overline{\Phi x}$): this exception makes the phallic function bearable because there is one to whom it does not apply. For those in the position of $\overline{\exists x}\ \overline{\Phi x}$, however, the $\overline{\forall x}\ \Phi x$ does not *per se* function as an exception: there is no equivocation between the two positions on the feminine side as there is on the masculine. Instead, the relationship between the two is conditional: one is the condition of the other, but one does not determine the other.

So what does this mean for understanding the $\overline{\exists x}\ \overline{\Phi x}$? Drawing on the work of Žižek (2005), I would suggest that this position represents the barred Other *par excellence*. As Žižek notes, the barred Other "carries within it an ex-timate, non-symbolisable kernel" (p. 13), but it is none-theless a desiring Other. This position, referred to as the *no exception*, then, is most definitely one occupied by a speakingbeing subject to the phallic function, but a speakingbeing that is nonetheless not fully within it, there is something about their relationship to it that is ex-timate (a term Lacan coined to refer to something that is both inside and outside at once). The position of the no exception is possible precisely because it is part of an open set: it is not defined by a limit case. Differ-ent to the $\overline{\forall x}\ \Phi x$, for which the speakingsubject in this position exceeds the phallic function in a specific way, the speakingbeing located in the position of the $\overline{\exists x}\ \overline{\Phi x}$ is one who may not act as though their jouissance is anything other than phallic (so may appear like the $\forall x\ \Phi x$), but for whom underneath this semblance of being limited to phallic jouissance there is a non-symbolisable part of their jouissance that is other.

With all of the above points in mind, we can again revisit Lacan's formula of sexuation and label each of the positions as follows:

Finite Equivocation	*Infinite Conditional*
Exception	No Exception
For-all	Not-all

Having now outlined Lacan's formula of sexuation, it is necessary to discuss how individual speakingbeings are located on one side or another, and where they are located within each side.

Sexuation and object a

Hopefully the reader will already have gleaned from the previous sec-tion the overall message of this chapter, namely that the matter which concerns us in terms of sexuation is not *per se* our bodies which are assigned with a particular sex, nor the bodies to whom we might be attracted which are also assigned a particular sex. This is not to say that bodies are moot, nor is it to say that conscious identifications or the meanings ascribed to particular bodies are moot. As I noted in the first chapter, clearly social norms impact upon how people experience themselves, and clearly there are considerable prohibitions placed on bodies and identities that are seen as outside the norm. Rather, the case I have been building in this chapter is that, analytically speaking, what concerns us are how speakingbeings make a choice as masculine or feminine, as part of a finite set that only has access to phallic jouissance, or as identified with an other jouissance that is both entirely within the phallic function whilst also accessing an other form of jouissance that is perhaps beyond phallic jouissance.

This brings me back to the point I made in the first chapter in regards to my own analysis. I noted that—at least on the surface—one of my questions appeared to me to be "why am I gay?" which more accurately might have been "what am I for a man or a woman?". Thinking about this question in terms of Lacan's formula of sexuation, we might instead reframe the question as four interrelated questions: 1) "what does it mean for me to be a speakingbeing?", 2) "what type of jouissance do I access?", 3) "what is the fantasy in which my jouissance circulates?", and 4) "how did the answers to the first three questions come to be as they are?". Lacan's formula of sexuation provides an answer to these four questions, and the manner by which we answer these questions potentially holds true for all speakingbeings.

The answer to these questions lies largely in the realm of the object *a*. The proposal I am making is a clarification or extension of our understanding of the operations of the object *a*. As I elaborated earlier, the object *a* are the leftovers or excess that remains once the child has entered into language. Ellie Ragland summarises the object *a* well, in stating:

> While individuals love others and things by investing jouissance in them [...] it is not the person or thing in itself that Lacan stressed, but the links or unary traits left over from loss of the primordial objects that first caused the infant to desire something or someone. In this sense, the object (*a*) is the pointillism of everyday life: a particular scent, or a lilt of the voice, that elicit desire in the infant's effort to retrieve a part of the lost object. But from the start, there is this paradox: The *object* that causes desire is not the actual thing the infant—and later the adult—wants. The traits are real, but the objects sought are symbolic or imaginary lure objects. Whether infant or adult, one desires the particularity of the conditions of enjoyment that initially linked the subject as a subject of desire ($) to the fantasy objects he or she later imagines can fill his lack and confer on him or her the homeostatic constancy of Oneness. (2004, p. 37)

The question that arises from any definition of object *a*, however, is why certain object *a* come into play, and what purpose they serve. My answer to this question is that, at least in part, they are determined by, and serve the purpose of, according the speakingbeing a position in relation to the first and second Other, and more specifically, that we hold onto them unconsciously as they allow us a fantasy in which we are able to overcome the fact of the sexual non-relationship—that we can experience a fantasised sense of oneness.

In Lacan's writing, the child is seen as identifying as either the lover or beloved of the first Other, who is taken as occupying a particular sexuated position and representing the object *a*. What, at least in my reading, appears less clearly addressed, is how the child determines this position. The answer that I have come to is that the child's position is determined in relation to how they decipher the first Other's own position as either masculine or feminine in terms of Lacan's formula of sexuation. Importantly, I am not suggesting that for each person a certain way of being for the Other naturally coalesces into one of the four modes outlined in Lacan's formula of sexuation (i.e., exception, for-all, not-all, no exception). Rather, my suggestion is that a child's location within one of these modes is determined by their deciphering of the position of their first Other within one of these modes, and how they then choose to position themselves in terms of sexuation so that they can sustain a fantasy in which they can keep their object *a* in circulation, and hence overcome the sexual non-relationship.

It is important to repeat the point here that Lacan's formula of sexuation is not a binary system. Whilst there is the finite mode of phallic jouissance and the infinite mode of an other jouissance, this does not mean they are oppositional. Thus to suggest, for example, that a child's caregiver is located in the position of the not-all, does not automatically mean that the child must be located within one of the two masculine positions. In formal logic certain positions within a logical square are contrary to, compatible with, implied in, or contradictory to one another. As can be seen in the following logical square as presented by Le Gaufey (2005), only one particular relationship is compatible (in terms of Lacan's formula of sexuation this would be the for-all and the not-all). Of course a child's sexuation does not have to be logically compatible to their caregiver's: it could be contradictory or contrary to it, or perhaps more opaquely, implied by it.

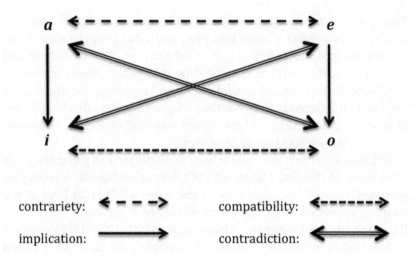

The important point to remember is that what we are discussing are structural positions within language. How a child deciphers their first Other's position within language potentially bears no relation to how the caregiver or other adults interpret their own position. What matters is that the child seeks to locate themselves in a relationship to their first Other, and in so doing to be their lover or beloved and thus hold onto a fantasy in which they can overcome the sexual non-relationship. How this fits with the object *a*, at least in my interpretation, is that the object *a* potentially tell us something about how the child deciphers the caregiver's desire, so far as the child understands it. The child's deciphering of their first Other's desire (and thus lack) is determined by how the first Other is viewed in a relationship to knowledge and jouissance, hence their location within Lacan's formula of sexuation. How the child goes about accessing the object *a* through a particular fantasy, I would then suggest, tells us something about the position they have adopted as a "solution" or "choice" in terms of being either the lover or beloved of the caregiver. It is the child's deciphering of their first Other's desire that I further outline in this section, before moving on in the following section to discuss how the child goes about attempting to access this desire through fantasy.

The work of Colette Soler is perhaps the most instructive in terms of understanding how the child interprets the position of the first Other. There are two ways in which Soler accounts for how the position of the first Other is interpreted. The first of these relates closely to the argument that I have presented above, namely in terms of how the child deciphers their first Other's desire. As Soler states:

> Desire that is specifically feminine makes the mother absent to her child, but for the child there will be a big difference in whether this absence is deciphered within the phallic order or whether, on the contrary, it will obscurely exceed this order. From the fact that phallicism speaks and is conveyed in signs, it establishes between objects an order in which the child tries to situate him/herself, even if only as a negative value. On the other hand, the *not-whole* remains, by definition, silent; it is an absolute silence that haunts everything that is ordered in the phallic series. (2006, p. 121)

It is somewhat unclear from this quote (and the text that surrounds it) whether the "desire that is specifically feminine" references the child's desire or (in this instance) the mother's desire. I take Soler to be talking about the latter, given the quote comes from a chapter section titled "The Mother, Other". With this in mind, it appears that Soler is suggesting that if the mother's desire is deciphered as being on the feminine side of the formula of sexuation, then the mother will appear absent to the child. It would appear that Soler then suggests that if the mother's feminine sexuation is deciphered as within the phallic order, then they will be in the position of the no-exception, $\overline{\exists x}\,\overline{\Phi x}$. If, however, the mother's feminine sexuation is deciphered as "obscurely exceed[ing the phallic] order", then they will be in the position of the not-all, $\overline{\forall x}\,\Phi x$.

I would extrapolate from these points made by Soler (2006) to suggest that a child may also decipher the mother as present, either in the form of the omnipresent exception to the phallic function, $\exists x\,\overline{\Phi x}$, or as the one who is present like all masculine speakingbeings (other than the exception), $\forall x\,\Phi x$. This extrapolation appears warranted by another piece of Soler's writing, in which she suggests that "The masculine identifies with a complete Other, while the feminine identifies with an incomplete øther" (2006 p. 124). This quote from Soler adds an important second vantage point from which to view how the child deciphers the caregiver's desire, specifically by emphasising that a child's deciphering occurs in the context of both the first Other's desire and the second Other's "no" (which the child takes as a cipher for understanding what it is that the first Other desires).

Having noted the importance of Soler's thinking on the topic, I would raise a few concerns about the potential that exists for the categories male and masculine sexuation, and female and feminine sexuation, to be collapsed into two binary categories. It would be far too easy to read the second quote from Soler above as suggesting that a child who chooses a masculine sexuation does so through identification with a masculine (i.e., complete) Other, who prohibits access to the desire of an Other who it could be implied is necessarily not masculine. I don't think this is necessarily Soler's intention, but the salience of gender categories and the association of masculinity with men and femininity with women can make it possible to read that Soler is talking about a male child and his father as differentiated from the mother. It is important as we progress in this book to bear in mind that this is neither my intent, nor presumably Soler's. Instead, the utility of Soler's account as I read it is to understand that a child comes to read the first Other's desire both through their own relation to their first Other, but also through the second Other's relationship to the first Other and the specific prohibitions they place on access to the first Other's desire, and that these are structural positions we are talking about, not gendered identities.

Sexuation and fantasy

In the final part of this chapter, I turn to examine the role of fantasy in sustaining access to the object a as a proxy for the sexual non-relationship. In so doing I provide an account alluded to earlier in regards to how the child, who believes they have deciphered the desire of the caregiver, can then hold onto that desire, thus giving them access to the sense of oneness they believe they have lost. To access that desire they make a choice of sexuation that best locates them in a relationship to the desire of their first Other.

As I noted above, at its most simple we can understand the position that the child adopts as being either one in which they are the beloved of the first Other, or they are the lover of the first Other. These two positions are typically associated with the masculine or feminine choice of sexuation, with the lover ($) located on the masculine side, and the beloved (a) located on the feminine side. This is rendered clearly in the mathemes that supplement Lacan's formula of sexuation.

Masculine	Feminine
$\exists x\ \overline{\Phi x}$ $\forall x\ \Phi x$	$\overline{\overline{\exists x}\ \overline{\Phi x}}$ $\overline{\forall x}\ \Phi x$

$\$$ \qquad\qquad $S(\cancel{A})$

a \qquad The

Φ

Whilst we might broadly concur with this division of the two positions, it is highly important that we remember that the bar that separates the masculine from the feminine is indeed a bar—commerce between the two sides is impossible, which is precisely the point of Lacan's statement that "there is no sexual relationship". Thus whilst there is some utility in understanding the choice of sexuation as one between being the lover or being the beloved, this really only tells one part of the story. For one, it only makes available two positions (beloved or lover), and further, it again all too easily slips into notions of active and passive, male and female, which is antithetical to the account of sexuation provided by Lacan. Silvia Rodríguez (1995) notes that in fact there are four positions available (exception, for-all, not-all, no-exception), and it is this suggestion that I take as central here.

Another important point to note about the table above is the fact that the object *a* is located on the side of the feminine. In reading in preparation to write this book I spent a considerable amount of time trying to identify the logic behind the mathemes that supplement the formula. Whilst Le Gaufey's discussion of formal logic was vital to understanding the formula, I could find little (either in Lacan's work or in the work of those who interpret him) that could help explain specifically the location of the object *a* on the feminine side. My concern arising from this was that I often found in my reading that when the mathemes are evoked, it is often in discussions about the child's choice of sexuation as either lover or beloved, always in relationship to the mother who is positioned in the location of the beloved object *a*, and hence on the side of the feminine (e.g., Ragland, 1995). This runs directly counter to the argument I am presenting in this chapter. For a long period of time I questioned whether the argument I have developed here was actually sound, primarily due to my inability to account for the location of the object *a* on the side of the feminine.

My conclusion is that, as with any of us who work with Lacan's writing, there has to be some give and take: there cannot be a clear answer to every twist and turn of his work. Someone else may read this book and have an immediate answer to my comments above, and I welcome such a response and engagement. In the context of this book, however, I take as important the fact that the mathemes do not clearly map across to the formula: the four positions outlined in the formula are not simply replicated as mathemes in the bottom half. Nor do the mathemes give us a set of coordinates through which particular sexuated positions relate to one another. Like other parts of Lacan's work, then, I leave to one side this particular aspect of his account of sexuation, focusing instead on the logical formulas provided in the top half. Such an approach encourages us to stay within the realms of logical positions with a structure, a structure centrally organised around desire (the deciphered desire of the caregiver, and the child's desire to be what the caregiver desires, both of which are shaped by messages the child receives about the caregiver's desire, particularly with relation to the "no" of the father).

As I suggested above, it is perhaps the role of fantasy that best gives us some traction in terms of identifying how desire is negotiated. As Žižek suggests:

> A fantasy constitutes our desire, provides its coordinates, i.e., it literally "teaches us how to desire". This role of fantasy hinges on the fact that "there is no sexual relationship", no universal formula or matrix guaranteeing a harmonious sexual relationship with one's partner. On account of the lack of this universal formula, every individual has to invent a fantasy of his or her own, a "private" formula for the sexual relationship. (1999, p. 191)

Importantly, the role of fantasy is not to give us access to our desire *per se*. To have our desire—to have access to jouissance—is anxiety producing, as Lacan (2014) noted. Instead, the role of fantasy is to keep desire in play—to keep it circulating so that our objects *a* allow us to maintain a belief in the possibility of oneness. In regards to our focus here on the role of fantasy in sexuation, Žižek suggests that fantasy is not simply about what we believe we don't have but want to believe we can have— a sense of oneness—but rather it explains why we *don't* have it:

> Fantasy provides a *rationale* for the inherent deadlock of desire; it gives a reason to the enigma of why "there is no sexual relationship". Fantasy is thus not simply the fantasy of a sexual relationship, but rather the fantasy of why it went wrong. It constructs the scene in which the jouissance we are deprived of is concentrated in the Other, who stole it from us. (1999, pp. 210, emphasis in original)

The final part of this quote, I would suggest, gives a significant access point in terms of how fantasy shapes our choice in terms of sexuation. If, as Žižek suggests, the blame for the loss of jouissance is to be attributed to the Other, then the fantasy in which our objects *a* circulates provides a map as to what deprived us of our jouissance (i.e., the "no" of the father), and what this deprivation has to tell us about the desire of the first Other, access to which we are denied. Our fundamental fantasy thus accords us a position from which we can reach the desire that is denied to us—it tells us where we need to be positioned in order to approximate the position of our first Other. Again, this is not in the form of a series of paired opposites, but rather in the form of a fantasy, the syntax of which allows us to maintain a belief in a fantasised oneness.

When we come to analysing fantasy in order to identify the routing of desire and what it can tell us about sexuation—as will be the task of the following six chapters—it is important to remember that what we are looking for is not *per se* how the speakingbeing appears in a fantasy as a mimicry of their conscious self. Rather, what we are looking for are how the signifiers of desire as they appear in the unconscious relay to us the position that the speakingbeing occupies. Both Darian Leader (2000) and Laplanche and Pontalis (1986) elaborate this most clearly in their discussions of Freud's account of children's beating fantasies. As the latter note:

> Fantasy, however, is not the object of desire, but its setting. In fantasy the subject does not pursue the object or its sign: he appears

caught up in himself in the sequence of images. He forms no representation of the desired object, but is himself represented as participating in the scene although, in the earliest forms of fantasy, he cannot be assigned any fixed place in it (hence the danger, in treatment, of interpretations which claim to do so). As a result, the subject, although always present in the fantasy, may be so in a des-ubjectivised form, that is to say, in the very syntax of the sequence in question. (p. 26)

As such, what we are looking for when analysing the dreams, slips, jokes, and forgettings of analysands—or in the case of this book, those elaborated by Freud in his case studies—is their place as a signifier within the operations of the objects a. Importantly, what we are also looking for, and what I believe is a relatively novel contribution of this book, is the place of the analysand's first and second Other, at least so far as the patient has deciphered them to be. Importantly, the aim in doing this is not to *per se* develop a taxonomy of which of the four positions within Lacan's formula of sexuation relate to one another most frequently. This type of formulisation would not necessarily add anything to the analytic encounter, and certainly may lead to prescriptive approaches to analytic practice that reduce any patient's analysis to a routine search for positions. Thus as Ellie Ragland notes:

> Even though the words one speaks (S_2), one's knowledge, *hide* unconscious traits (S_1), some part of these details can still be recuperated through attention to the *lettre* or drive signifier because they coalesce around what Lacan called the object-cause-of-desire. Indeed, the structure of fantasy ($\$ \lozenge a$) denotes just this: The subject is pushed by (unconscious) desire to seek something lost as a substitute for the first object-*cause*-of-desire. Desire resides in the fantasy as lack because the object (a), denoting the radically lost object-of-desire, can only refind itself in the traces of jouissance in the signifier, in an image, or in affect. (2004, p. 72, emphasis in original)

As we will see in the chapters to come, and different to the majority of readings that have been made of Freud's cases, any individual's choice in regards to sexuation cannot be easily determined by focusing on their identifications nor the gender of their object choices. Rather, what is required is engaging in a complex examination of positionings in which the individual's deciphering of the desire of the first Other instructs (though importantly does not lead to in the sense of a one-to-one correspondence with) their own desire. Such an approach thus closely aligns with Lacan's repeated point that our desire is the desire of the Other.

Conclusions

I will of course repeatedly return to the argument I have presented in this chapter in the following chapters. To summarise it here, however, the key points of the theoretical framework I have developed in this chapter are that:

1. It is useful in terms of examining sexuation because it doesn't rely upon identification with a particular person marked by their assigned sex. Such a reliance upon identification with a mother or father who is seen *as a* woman or man (the presumed correlation being *as a* feminine or masculine person) is an approach to psychoanalytic writing that I have seen time and time again, and which I think is a fundamental misunderstanding of Lacan's work (and certainly I am far from the first to say this, see Ragland, 2004; Soler, 2006). As those who interpret Lacan's work already know, the child assumes that because there is a certain correspondence between a mother and father (in the case where they have both, or only one of each), that there is a correspondence between women and men. As Lacan has extensively argued, and as I have summarised in this chapter, this correspondence is an illusion: there is no sexual rapport.

2. It emphasises the speakingbeing's object *a*, though importantly with a different intent to Dean (2000). Very broadly speaking, Dean navigates something of a similar path to my own in terms of emphasising the role of the object *a* in understanding desire. His path, however, is one that is guided by a desire to replace Lacan's emphasis on the phallus with an emphasis on the object *a*. There is certainly much merit to Dean's argument, but for me Lacan's formula of sexuation—which is centrally about the phallic function (all speakingbeings are subject to the phallic function by the very fact of their entrance into language and the "no" of the father)—has a lot to offer in terms of understanding the relationship between sexuation, the object *a*, and fantasy. That both Dean and I see great

importance in continuing to focus on the object *a* signals, I think, that we are both on the right track. That one of us continues to accept the utility of working with the phallic function and one of use challenges the centrality of the phallus I think is simply a matter of different agendas and aims. For me, as I will explore in the final chapter of this book, working with the formula of sexuation through fantasy and the object *a* gives considerable purchase in the clinic.

3. Whilst not outlined in any great detail in this chapter, by the time we get to the final chapter of the book it will be possible to see, as I have suggested above, that the approach I have outlined in this chapter provides us with ways not only to understand the structural positionings of the analysand (and their first and second Other), but also how the analyst fits within all of this. As I will discuss in the final chapter, how the analysand positions the analyst structurally has significant implications for the functioning of the transference and thus the treatment.

In each of the following analytic chapters I first introduce the case itself, before then summarising a selection of previous accounts of the case (both those that I potentially disagree with, and those that offer some insight in terms of my examination of the case), following which I present my account of sexuation in each case. By working through six of Freud's cases in this way, I will demonstrate in considerable detail the applicability of the theoretical framework presented in this chapter.

CHAPTER TWO

The psychogenesis of a case of homosexuality in a woman

The case

Arguably, Freud's (1920a) "The psychogenesis of a case of homosexuality in a woman" has received the least attention in psychoanalytic literature (though see chapters in Lesser & Schoenberg, 1999). Yet as we will see in the following section, the attention it has received positions it as a useful first case to examine in this book, given the emphasis placed in previous accounts upon the analysand's position in terms of sexuation. Before moving on to review a selection of previous accounts of the case, however, it is important to first consider the case itself.

Patricia Gherovici (2010) informs us that in chronicling the life of the young women who was the focus of case, Rieder and Voigt (2003) use the pseudonym Sidonie Csillag, though it was disclosed after her death in 1999 that her real name was Margarethe Trautenegg. As is the case with some of Freud's other cases, the truth of the matter (with regard to names, biographical details, and outcomes) is somewhat opaque. For the purposes of this chapter I will work with the pseudonym given by Rieder and Voigt, given the fact that this will be familiar to at least some readers, and seems more satisfactory that referring to the analysand as "the young homosexual woman" (as has typically been the case in previous writing).

From the outset of his account Freud is keen to emphasise a number of key points about the analysis. First, Sidonie was brought to see Freud by her father, who refused to accept his daughter's homosexuality, and who wished for Freud to "correct it". Freud is clear in his reporting of the case that this was never likely to happen, and in general is seldom likely to be possible in any case. In addition to the fact that Sidonie came to see Freud not *per se* of her own volition, Freud notes that Sidonie came without symptoms, which was atypical in regards to an analysis. Given these two prohibiting factors, it is never quite clear why Freud agreed to take on the case. One reason might be the marginalised status of psychoanalysis in Vienna at the time (a fact that Freud comments on in the case). Freud might reasonably have needed to take on a paying client. Another reason, and one that Freud emphasises from the very beginning of his report of the case, is that working with Sidonie could provide him with the opportunity to theorise about homosexuality. Whilst this makes Freud appear to be something of an opportunist, at the same time it says something about his recognition of the fact that there was something to be said about homosexuality (specifically in the case of women). Whether or not the theory he derived from the case is particularly accurate, useful, or non-pathologising has since been the topic of much debate (see chapters in Lesser & Schoenberg, 1999, specifically those written by Fuss and de Lauretis).

With these disclaimers in place, Freud is able to outline the details of the case in relatively few pages. Primarily this is because the analysis only lasted a matter of months, but also because, it would appear, Sidonie did not provide him with a great amount of detail to work with (and indeed Gherovici, 2010, suggests that much of the detail Freud had to work with may have come from Sidonie's father). At its simplest, Sidonie's journey up until the point of the analysis had involved what Freud argues to be a life-long homosexual orientation, played out through Sidonie's attractions to a range of women (mothers at the park, an actress at a summer resort, and at the time of the analysis, a "Lady" of ill repute who nonetheless held a relatively high social standing). Her homosexuality was not a problem for Sidonie herself, though it was a problem for her father (and for a lesser extent her mother). Sidonie shared something of a close relationship with her mother, and a combative relationship with her father. Sidonie had one older brother (whom Freud suggests Sidonie had an attraction to, though this is never substantiated), and two younger brothers, the youngest of whom Freud suggests precipitated a crisis in Sidonie's life. Specifically, Freud suggests that whilst Sidonie's homosexuality pre-dated the birth of her youngest brother, it was only upon his birth that she started actively pursuing the Lady mentioned above.

Sidonie's relationship with the Lady in question was perhaps the key issue that brought her to Freud. Not only in relation to homosexuality, but also in relation to a suicide attempt. Freud notes that whilst the Lady was much adored by Sidonie, the Lady did little to reciprocate her feelings, other than occasionally allowing Sidonie to give her a chaste kiss on the hand. This apparently changed to a degree following a suicide attempt by Sidonie. This was precipitated, Freud suggests, by a particular interaction between Sidonie, her father, and the Lady. On one particular day Sidonie was out walking with the Lady, in an area where her father frequented. Freud reports that Sidonie's father saw her, glared at her, and Sidonie then rushed off and leaped over a railing surrounding a cut in the street that led to a tram track below. Sidonie survived the leap, though had to spend a considerable amount of time recovering.

An important final part of the story is elaborated by Gherovici (2010), who notes that it wasn't simply the glare from her father that potentially precipitated her leap onto the tram tracks. Following the glare (and before her leap), the Lady had stated to Sidonie that she was done with the relationship. This seems important to emphasise: that it was potentially both the father's glare *and* the Lady's rejection that led to Sidonie's leap onto the tram tracks. Either way, Freud notes that after her recovery, not only were Sidonie's parents somewhat more kindly disposed towards her, but this was also true in regards to the Lady.

With this brief summary of the case provided, we can now turn to examine what other writers have made of the case.

Previous accounts

As I noted above, less has been written about "The psychogenesis of a case of homosexuality in a woman" than has been written about Freud's other cases. That said, what has been written about this case is of direct relevance to my argument in this book, perhaps more than is true of writings about Freud's other cases (with the case of Dora being a notable exception). Some of that which has been written about the case constitutes what I suggested in chapter one to be a simplistic example of a pink herring. In regards to Sidonie, this is not to suggest that she was not homosexual, but rather to suggest that accusations made against Freud in regards to the case (i.e., that he was homophobic or anti-lesbian) are somewhat misguided.

Perhaps the clearest example of this is in the work of Fuss (1993). I must say up front that it is difficult for me to position the work of Fuss in this instance as misguided, as I have always enjoyed her work. In this case, however, the account that Fuss provides of the case is highly skewed by the fact that it seems to treat as an *a priori* Freud's non-acceptance of lesbianism, or at the very least seems to view Freud as collapsing female homosexuality into male homosexuality (an argument also made by de Lauretis, 1994). These concerns about Fuss' argument aside, the account provided by Fuss sets up a binary of masculinity and femininity that is antithetical to the premise of this book. Fuss argues that whilst Freud suggests that Sidonie had made a masculine identification with her father (which Fuss sees as Freud's explanation for Sidonie's homosexuality), Sidonie's "suicide plunge" (p. 16) suggests a feminine identification with her mother (in that it was an attempt at gaining her father's positive regard). Fuss also suggests that Freud's argument about the Lady as love object is inadequate, in that, by Fuss' estimation, Freud does not adequately clarify the "gendered identity" of the love object (p. 16).

As the theoretical outline presented in chapter two would suggest, this type of simplistic account of identification and object choice as imputed to Freud by Fuss (1993) is inadequate to understanding what exactly was at stake for Sidonie, both with regard to her love for the Lady, and in regard to her leap onto the tram tracks. Without pre-empting the following section too much, I would argue that basing any argument about Sidonie's identification or the "gender identity" of her love object upon the assigned sex of any of the players in the drama (i.e., Sidonie, her mother, her father, and the Lady) will always limit how far we may proceed in understanding the issues at stake.

Jacobus (1995) too emphasises the idea that Sidonie displayed a feminine as opposed to masculine identification, albeit by a different logic to that reported by Fuss (1993) and with considerably less animosity towards Freud. In her account of Sidonie's love for the Lady, Jacobus argues that for Freud, instances of "passion" are seen as feminine, rather than masculine. Jacobus emphasises the comparison between Freud's report that Sidonie resembled her father in so far as her "intellectual attributes" (p. 68) were devoid of passion, whilst her passion for the Lady was feminine. As Jacobus states:

> In Freud's gender scheme it is masculine to desire the lady, but fem-
> inine to make a virile display of phallic desire. Loving a woman as
> a man might do [...] takes on the paradoxical appearance of femi-
> ninity. (p. 68)

Whilst the argument that Jacobus presents is perhaps a plausible inter-pretation of Freud's account, it nonetheless is limited by its reliance upon the normative assumption that any person's desire for a woman is automatically masculine (as though femininity and masculinity were paired opposites), and by its somewhat odd suggestion that "loving a woman as a man might do" (i.e., show passion) "takes on the paradoxi-cal appearance of femininity", given this would suggest that any per-son assigned male at birth who shows passion for a woman gives the appearance of femininity—this would seem a bold claim to make.

Again emphasising an account of the case that focuses on mascu-linity and femininity as paired opposites, Watson (2013) argues that Sidonie adopts a masculine position in regards to her father. As Watson suggests, Sidonie loves the Lady—who is presumed to be feminine by default of her assignation as female—as a masculine person. Whilst in her account Watson states that this should not be mistaken for any desire on Sidonie's part to become a man, and whilst Watson adopts a Lacanian approach to the topic, she nonetheless reduces a masculine position to one that involves "desiring like a man" (p. 18), as though all speakingbeings located on the masculine side of the formula of sexua-tion were assigned male at birth, with homosexual women thus being speakingbeings who only approximate men who, by default it would seem, desire "like men". Whilst different from Fuss' (1993) account (in that Watson deploys the work of Lacan to read the case), there is none-theless a similarity in the way that subject positions are reduced, at least implicitly, to bodies—hence Watson locates Sidonie's masculine posi-tioning as being "like a man".

Hamer (1990) critiques these types of account of female homosex-uality, and suggests that in reading Freud as establishing female homosexuality as a matter of male identification, this effectively renders lesbian desire moot. In other words, as Hamer suggests, the "masculine lesbian" who desires a women like herself is prohibited from desire (given both women will be "on the same side of desire", p. 147). Conversely, "masculine lesbians" who desire "feminine women" will only be desired by such women "as men". Hamer goes into detail about why this type of interpretation of Freud is incorrect, however what she doesn't then do is provide an account of female homosexuality that *per se* makes lesbian desire possible in terms of sexuation. Whilst, as I outlined in chapter one, doing this isn't necessarily the intention of this book (i.e., my interest is not to provide a "correct" reading of homosexuality that would be applicable to all people who identify as homosexual—this would be yet another pink herring), in the following section I do provide an account of sexuation in the case of Sidonie that at least provides us some coordinates for thinking about her desire as a sexuated subject. Whether or not this tells us anything about "women's desire" or "lesbian desire" more specifically is a topic I will return to in the final chapter of this book.

In addition to the Lacanian account provided by Watson (2013) outlined above, at least three other writers have engaged in Lacanian analyses of the case. Each of these, in differing ways, engages with Lacan's arguments about courtly love and their application to the relationship between Sidonie and the Lady. At its simplest, Lacan's account is that courtly love represented one way of attempting to overcome the fact of the sexual non-relation. As Lacan suggests, when the courtly lover—typically the minstrel—exalts their beloved to the status of the adored object, what they are doing is suggesting that were it not for their position of worship, their beloved would be accessible to them.

Writers such as Ellie Ragland (1995) have suggested that it is precisely a form of courtly love that Sidonie engages in. Ragland suggests that by refraining from engaging in intimacy with the Lady (other than the odd chaste kiss on the hand), and by sending her flowers and other displays of adoration, Sidonie exalts the Lady to the position of the beloved. In so doing, Sidonie allows for her desire to remain in play, as some part of the Lady represents the object *a* that circulates within Sidonie's fantasy.

Van Haute and Geyskens (2012), however, offer a slightly different interpretation of Sidonie's relationship to the Lady in regards to courtly love. They differentiate courtly love from the adoration that Sidonie showed towards the Lady. They suggest that:

> Unlike in either hysteria or the case of the homosexual young
> woman, courtly love radicalises unsatiability neither to fend some-
> thing off (hysteria), nor as an attempt to earn something to which
> one continues to feel entitled (the case of the homosexual young
> woman). Courtly love sings the praises of the structural impossibil-
> ity of desire's fulfilment and it does so by way of the lady's *ideali-*
> *sation*, which puts her out of reach. (Van Haute & Geyskens, 2012,
> p. 115)

Following Ragland, I would question this depiction of Sidonie's adoration of the Lady as different to courtly love. As I will discuss further
in the next section of this chapter, I do not believe that Sidonie's goal
was to "attempt to earn something to which [she] continue[d] to feel
entitled". In fact, what I will suggest is that the object *a* that the Lady
represented was precisely something that Sidonie did not wish to earn,
for as Lacan (2014) suggests, anxiety comes into play precisely when the
speakingbeing gets too close to their objects *a*—the latter operate within
a fantasy that needs to remain as such.

The reading of the case that is perhaps the closest to my own is that
provided by Gherovici (2010). In her reading, Gherovici maps out how
the object *a* that the Lady represented spoke of Sidonie's structural relationship with her mother and father in terms of sexuation. Different
from my own reading, however, Gherovici suggests that in deferring
to her mother (by identifying as homosexual—thus leaving men for her
mother), Sidonie viewed her mother as the $\exists x \, \overline{\Phi x}$, as the exception to
the law of castration on the masculine side of the formula of sexua-
tion. From this, Gherovici suggests that Sidonie "sacrificed her 'normal'
femininity and chose an angelic femininity" (p. 128). As we will see
now, the reading I provide of the case argues for a somewhat different account of sexuation as it pertains to Sidonie, her mother, and her
father.

A focus on sexuation

Before presenting my interpretation of the case in terms of a focus on
sexuation, let us first briefly recap my argument from chapter two. In
that chapter, through an extensive engagement with Lacan's formula of
sexuation, I made the case that a person's structural position in terms of
sexuation is determined by how they decipher the structural position

of their first Other; how that is in some ways "revealed" to them by the "no" of the second Other; and how the positions of all three (analysands, their first Other and their second Other) can be identified through the operations of the analysand's fantasy and the objects a that circulate within it. In the case of Sidonie (as with the cases that follow in subsequent chapters), then, what we are attempting to identify are structural positions and their relationship to objects a. This process of identifying, as is often the case in Lacanian psychoanalysis, travels in multiple directions. As much as a person's deciphering of their first Other's structural position will determine the fantasy that permits them access to their object a, the object a as psychical remainders of an imagined oneness before the cut into language will determine how the speaking-being deciphers the structural position of the first Other.

With this summary in mind, it might perhaps be easiest if I clearly state here what I believe are the positions indicated within the case, before then unpacking in detail why I believe this to be the case. By my reading—which like all readings is situated and partial—Sidonie deciphered her mother as being in the position of the no exception $\overline{\forall x}\ \Phi x$, and her father as being in the position of the exception $\exists x\ \overline{\Phi x}$. Sidonie, I would suggest, occupies the position of the for-all $\forall x\ \Phi x$. Let us now explore in detail the argument that led me to these conclusions.

Much of Freud's discussion of the case rests upon the assumption that Sidonie had previously identified with her mother, and wanted her father to give her a child that would resemble him. When, instead, her mother became unexpectedly pregnant when Sidonie was sixteen, Freud argues, Sidonie became angry with her father, and in order to exact her vengeance upon him, took up with the Lady in order to usurp her father's masculine position. In my reading, whilst this account gives some coordinates for orientating our understanding of Sidonie's sexuation, it situates them in the wrong place, thus constituting a pink herring in this case.

First, I would argue that what Sidonie sought was not a child by her father, but rather that her mother would have a child by her. This, I would suggest, was her fantasy—not that she is the exception who can have any woman, but rather that she is the for-all who can have each woman in turn one by one and for each to bear a child to her. We see this when Freud talks over a matter of pages about a list of women to whom Sidonie had shown affection over the years: an actress, some young mothers in the park, and at the time of the analysis, the Lady.

What Sidonie sought in these women was not *per se* them as women (though this is not to deny that she might have identified consciously as homosexual). Rather, what she sought in these women was the fact that they *could* bear a child to her.

What is most important here to state very clearly is that it is the *capacity* of a woman to bear a child to Sidonie that was at stake, not the actual birth of a child. This is important as what is at stake, then, is not the incest taboo that the exception can violate—Sidonie having sex with her mother—but rather that a woman could bear a child *for* her. Freud states something to this effect: "At the time of the analysis the idea of pregnancy and child-birth was disagreeable to her, partly, I surmise, on account of the bodily disfigurement connected with them" (1920a, p. 169). Again, I think here the coordinates of Sidonie's desire require some reconfiguring. It would seem far too simplistic—especially with regard to a man such as Freud for whom things were rarely taken at surface value—to accept that pregnancy was actually disagreeable to Sidonie. Perhaps consciously as a young woman, yes, becoming pregnant might have seemed distasteful, as may well have been the case for many young women at the time. Nonetheless, we must wonder about whether the "disagreeable" nature of pregnancy masked the fact that a pregnancy was desirable, albeit one undertaken by another person.

Freud himself makes precisely this argument in the paper "A special type of object choice made by men" (1910h), where he suggests:

> The mother gave the child life, and it is not easy to find a substitute of equal value for this unique gift. With a slight change of meaning, such as is easily effected in the unconscious and is comparable to the way in which in consciousness concepts shade into one another, rescuing his mother takes on the significance of giving her a child or making a child for her—needless to say, one like himself. (p. 173)

In the case of Sidonie, then, perhaps part of her fantasy was structured by the idea of reciprocity to her mother—of giving her a child. Like any fantasy, however, this only works as a fantasy. For any fantasy to come into reality runs the risk of anxiety associated with coming too close to the objects *a* that circulate within and through the fantasy.

Having begun elaborating the case for seeing Sidonie as located in the position of the for-all, let us return to her mother and examine more closely her position as Sidonie may have understood it. Freud remarks in the case that Sidonie's mother's pregnancy came as something of a surprise, suggesting that whilst her mother was still a "youngish woman" (p. 149), it was nonetheless an unexpected pregnancy. In this regard, it is important to note the uneasy allegiance between Sidonie's views on pregnancy as conjectured by Freud, and his views of Sidonie's mother as a person who "enjoyed her daughter's confidence concerning her passion", who only objected to her daughter's homosexuality should it impact upon the "great deal of consideration [she received] from her husband", and who was "over-indulgent to her three sons" (p. 149), though not to her daughter. This, at least in my reading, is a woman who is potentially positioned in the place of the no exception, as one who has access to an other jouissance that is ex-timate. Certainly, her awareness that "consideration from her husband" was contingent upon her concession to his views about their daughter would seem to indicate her submission to the phallic function. But at the same time, her indulgence of her sons, and her enjoyment in her daughter's passion, suggests perhaps that there was some other form of jouissance that she could access.

This deciphering of her mother as the no exception is perhaps also evident in the very fantasy itself, one of giving a child to her mother. Whilst much has been made, as per above, of the claim that Sidonie displayed a masculine identification and positioning, we might come to a different set of coordinates if we unpack this a little further. The previous accounts of the case that I initially summarised above emphasise Sidonie's positioning as "like a man", and in so doing conflate "being a man" with "being on the side of the masculine" in the formula of sexuation. If we instead view Sidonie as someone who was a young woman, but who in her fantasy believed she could give a child to her mother, then this enables us to conjecture about the positioning of her mother, perhaps more than it allows us to conjecture about Sidonie, at least in the first instance. If her mother—as someone assigned female—is someone who can be given a child by someone also assigned female, then her mother is positioned potentially as someone who has access to an other jouissance beyond the phallic. Admittedly, we are talking here at the level of the unconscious and not the physical act of reproduction, but nonetheless it is in fantasy that we see the operations of desire and what they can tell us about the coordinates of sexuation.

Finally in regards to the mother, we must look at the position of the father. What messages do the "no" of the father give about the mother's positioning? The father, I have suggested, appears to be positioned as the exception to the phallic function on the masculine side of the formula of the equation. Different to the fathers in many of Freud's other cases—fathers whose "no" was inadequate or which functioned in contradictory or unstable ways—Sidonie's father appeared to represent a "no" that everyone in the family took relatively seriously (even Sidonie it would seem, despite Freud's claim that she had relative disregard for her father's prohibitions on her love for the Lady). Whilst her father was not *per se* the exception who *has* all of the women, he was certainly a person who *could* have all that he wanted. Certainly it would seem that Sidonie attempted to destabilise his position as the exception, as Freud notes: "She *wanted* her father to know occasionally of her relations with the lady, otherwise she would be deprived of the satisfaction of her keenest desire—namely, revenge" (p. 159, emphasis in original). Yet her father's response was not that of the for-all, for whom the threat of castration is always on the horizon. Rather, his response was one of relative indifference: in the case of the suicide attempt, merely a glare before he was on his way. Someone who is not threatened by another's attempt at vengeance is someone who is beyond the law of the phallic function.

If the argument I have presented above about the structural positions of Sidonie's mother and father is accepted, then what place did Sidonie need to position herself in so as to be able to access the object *a* represented by her mother? At first glance it might seem that Sidonie went head to head with her father in an attempt at usurping his position of the exception, so as to claim that position for herself. Freud's reference to Sidonie as the "*grande dame*" who responded with the depreciating comment, "How very interesting" when presented with "a specially important part of the theory" (p. 163) could be read as Sidonie seeing herself as beyond the law of the phallic function. Furthermore, Freud notes that after her leap onto the tram tracks Sidonie was given considerable more leeway by her parents, and received renewed attention from the Lady. This too could suggest that Sidonie sought to position herself as the one who is the exception to the phallic function. This, however, would I think be a simplistic reading of these examples.

Instead I would suggest, as I did above, that Sidonie attempted to take women one-by-one, that as the for-all, there was nothing *per se* unique or exceptional about her ability to do this, but nonetheless as a speakingbeing located on the masculine side of the formula of sexuation she could nonetheless take women and in her fantasy give them a child. Importantly, however, what we are talking about here is fantasy. A fantasy functions precisely because it is not reality. But in relation to her mother Sidonie did, at least unconsciously I would suggest, give her mother a child. Taking up with the Lady, then, is not about a turning away from a father who failed to give her a child, but rather a turning away from a mother who brought into reality her fantasy. Freud states this specifically: "The analysis revealed beyond all shadow of doubt that the lady-love was a substitute for her mother" (p. 155). By my interpretation, however, the substitution was not *per se* for a "mother", but rather for a woman *who could be a mother*. The Lady thus represented a person who in fantasy Sidonie could give a child—physiologically the Lady was a person who could carry a child—but who was much less of a risk in comparison to her mother in terms of actually making this a reality.

The Lady, then, could be positioned by Sidonie in the place of the no exception, and in so doing could replace the role of her mother as the woman who could be gotten pregnant but whom would not. In regards to the positioning of the Lady as the no exception, this was a woman of "good birth" who was "forced into her present position only by adverse family circumstances". This was also a woman who "persistently rejected the girl's advances up to the time of the attempted suicide" (p. 152). This, then, was a speakingbeing who was subject to the phallic function (she was vulnerable to the "no" of the father in the form of family circumstances that could become adverse), but she was also someone who has access to an other form of jouissance. Despite people's judgements about her (including Sidonie's own parents), this was a person whose life was not wholly circumscribed by social mores. Similarly, this was a woman who despite compromised financial circumstances could say no to Sidonie's advances (which often included gifts).

In regards to the role of the Lady as a replacement for the mother as a woman who could be gotten pregnant but whom would not, Freud again makes comment on this. As he notes:

> It may seem remarkable that she was not in the least repelled by the bad reputation of her beloved, although her own observations sufficiently confirmed the truth of such rumours [...]. But already her first passions had been for women who were not celebrated for

especially strict propriety [...]. For her, the bad reputation of her "lady", however, was positively a "necessary condition for love". (p. 161)

The Lady was a woman whose source of income, it would appear, relied upon being able to engage in intimacy with men without becoming pregnant. Whilst this was no guarantee that she would never be pregnant, she certainly was a much more reliable place in which Sidonie could invest her fantasy of giving a child to a woman.

All of this discussion about the Lady and her role in fulfilling Sidonie's fantasy of giving a child to a woman brings us to a final point requiring elaboration, namely the role of her leap onto the tram tracks. In previous accounts of the case, including those made by Lacan (2014), much has been made of the fact that the word "fall" used by Freud references both physically falling (as Sidonie did onto the tram tracks), but also to fall pregnant. This, I would suggest here following Gherovici (2010), is something of a read herring. First, I would suggest that turning a "leap" into a "fall"—the word that Freud uses in discussing the action, despite the fact that in his initial description of the event he stated that she "flung herself into the railway cutting" (p. 162)—does something of a disservice to the act itself. It isn't as though Sidonie tripped over by accident and fell onto the tram track. Rather, she leapt, she jumped, she flung herself over the edge of the cut in the pavement and down on to the tram tracks below. To make this about Sidonie's desire to be pregnant is thus perhaps a rather simplistic and over determined interpretation of her "fall".

Nonetheless, and following Lacan (2014), we can agree that Sidonie's leap onto the tram tracks was indeed what he terms a passage-to-the-act. But the question then remains, what precisely was the leap intended to achieve if we treat it—as the notion of the "fall" does—as a metaphor? My suggestion here is that Sidonie's leap was about keeping her fantasy in play. Prior to the leap, the Lady had stated that she wished to end things with Sidonie. Ending the relationship would have prevented Sidonie having access to someone through whom she could access her fantasy of giving a child to a woman. Sidonie's leap, then, is a falling for someone else: she didn't want the Lady to get pregnant, nor did she want the Lady to not get pregnant (in the sense of breaking off the relationship and thus no longer serving the fantasy). Instead, Sidonie needed for her to remain as someone who could be gotten pregnant. The fall that Sidonie undertakes is thus a way of denying the sexual non relationship by showing that as the lover of the Lady she could fall for her, not so as to be pregnant herself, but so as to enact a falling on behalf of the Lady. This both allowed the fantasised pregnancy to remain in play, without anyone actually having to be pregnant. And of course at the conscious level, the leap itself was to a certain degree guaranteed to produce sympathy and positive regard from the Lady, which Freud reports was indeed the case.

Following others who have written about this case, we can impute another final meaning about falling in general within the case. Freud notes that before the analysis ended Sidonie had reported to him dreams that he felt suggested she was lying to him, or more correctly that her unconscious was lying. The contents of these dreams, Freud suggests, "confessed her longing for a man's love and for children" (p. 165). Freud, however, told Sidonie that he did not believe the dreams, and that they were intended to deceive him "just as she habitually deceived her father" (p. 165). Freud broke off treatment and advised Sidonie's parents that if they wished to pursue an analysis for Sidonie it should be with a female analyst. What can we make of this chain of events?

I would suggest perhaps that Sidonie's dreams—if they are indeed a form of deceit as Freud suggests—were aimed at denying Freud the position of the no exception, and thus refusing him a place in her fantasy. Without going into too much additional detail about the case, we might conjecture that for Sidonie, Freud was neither the exception who is not subject to the phallic function (the impoverished social opinion of psychoanalysis at the time would suggest as much), nor was he the for-all who could have his desire one at a time. Instead, we might suggest, to Sidonie he appeared as a speakingbeing who had access to an other jouissance, as indicated by the fact that whilst he experienced prohibitions on his analytic practice in terms of the low esteem in which it was held, he nonetheless continued to practice and to receive some positive regard (such as from her parents, who brought her to Freud in the first place). Having an analyst in the place of the exception—as someone structurally akin to the Lady—was likely not at all desirable for Sidonie, perhaps primarily because he was a man who could not be gotten pregnant (thus Freud was in the right structural position, but undermined the fantasy associated with the position). What Sidonie needed, then, was for Freud to fall. Not to fall pregnant *per se*, but to fall from his structural position. To deceive him and have him terminate the analysis was thus one way to move herself outside a relationship which threatened to undermine her fantasy. In the final chapter of this book I will take up in greater detail what this means in the regards to transference.

Conclusions

What I hope I have shown in this first chapter focusing on one of Freud's cases is that it is possible to discern something of the structural positionings of an analysand from their account of the positionings of their first and second Other. As I noted earlier, to a certain extent "The psychogenesis of a case of homosexuality in a woman" was a good case to start with as my analysis of it sits in a context of other accounts of the case which have, in varying ways, focused on sexuation. At the same time, however, due to the limited amount of analytic material provided in the Freud's account of the case, I have been limited to a large degree in regards to the attention I could give to the syntax of Sidonie's fantasy, relying instead on more general descriptors of Sidonie and her parents. I will be the first to acknowledge that whilst I believe the account I have provided of the positioning of Sidonie's mother and father is quite accurate, and whilst the terms of her fantasy would seem to be quite thoroughly expounded, my account of her object a and Sidonie's own positioning are somewhat less precise. Missing, then, is a focus on the syntax of her fantasy that would have helped to more precisely pinpoint her positioning and object a, and thus helped us to better understand how her fantasy allowed Sidonie to maintain a belief that she could overcome the sexual non-relationship.

In subsequent chapters, focusing on cases where Freud provided more analytic material (specifically dreams), we will see that the deciphering of sexuation I have provided in this first analytic chapter is extended when we are able to focus more closely on the syntax of fantasy. Specifically, such an extended focus allows us to see the complex location of the object a in fantasies that shore up a belief in the possibility of a oneness, at the same time as they ensure that this possibility is never actually tested.

CHAPTER THREE

From the history of an infantile neurosis

The case

In regards to Freud's (1918b) "From the history of an infantile neurosis", whilst Strachey suggests that it "is the most elaborate and no doubt the most important of all Freud's case histories" (p. 3), in my reading the case materials as provided by the analysand are actually quite thin. Most of what we have to go on, similar to much of what we have to go on with Little Hans as we shall see in chapter six, are Freud's constructions and the material that is then provoked from them. The similarity between the two cases is noted by Freud himself, and given the fact that almost all of "From the history of an infantile neurosis" focuses on the analysand's childhood before the age of five, the similarity is perhaps understandable.

Also notable about this case is the fact that whilst Freud refers to the analysand—Sergei Pankejeff—as phobic in his childhood, and as an obsessional in his adulthood, other authors have offered alternative diagnoses. Specifically, Davis (1995) has suggested that Sergei potentially had a psychotic structure due to the failure of the "no" of the father, though as we shall see later in this chapter, religion served as an alternative "no" to Sergei's actual father (though it has been suggested

37

that many years after his treatment by Freud, Sergei did indeed suffer psychotic delusions, which may be explained by the fact that the role of religion as the "no" of the father was to a certain degree inadequate). Other writers such as Abraham and Torok (1986) and Ferraro (2010) have suggested that Sergei displayed a perverse structure, with Abraham and Torok specifically making the case that the analysand Freud discusses in his writing on fetish who had a particular fondness for a "shine on the nose" was actually Sergei. Whilst this particular claim is very interesting, it is not, however, something that I will explore in this chapter, focusing instead with the materials presented in the case by Freud.

In terms of the case, and as I noted above, whilst Sergei presented to Freud for analysis as an adult, the analysis focused almost entirely on the first five years of his life. The time when Sergei presented for analysis was several years after an infection with gonorrhoea which at the time had put him in a state of considerable distress and which, whilst responding to a particularly harsh treatment, had continued to result in a state of psychological dependency upon others. As we shall see, however, Freud traces the events at the time of the analysis to the early years of Sergei's life, thus positioning the case as the greatest example of Freud's work on the infantile basis of adult neuroses.

With regard to his early life, we are told that Sergei grew up as a member of a wealthy Russian family, with estates in both the countryside and in a town. Both of his parents suffered from a range of physical illnesses, and Sergei and his sister were cared for in the large part by a succession of nannies, primarily an older Russian woman (but also a younger English woman, a point that is relevant to our discussion of the case to come). Freud suggests that Sergei was frequently terrorised by his older sister, particularly with regard to a storybook that included an image of a wolf depicted as walking upright on its hindquarters. It is from this image that Freud traces Sergei's dream about wolves that we will discuss below, and which resulted in the moniker "Wolf man" that is often appended to the case. In addition to this terrorising, Freud reports that Sergei was subject to sexual advances by his sister at a young age.

Despite all of this, Sergei reported to Freud that in his early years he was a relatively easy-going child, though this changed around the age of five, when he became prone to tantrums and anger. These, however, were gradually replaced over the following two years by religious piousness, which primarily involved ritualised prayers that were routinely blasphemous. In his early years Sergei was also plagued by bouts of faecal incontinence, which Freud maps onto his adult experience of constipation requiring enemas. Indeed, much of the case is preoccupied with what Freud takes to be Sergei's anal eroticism. As we shall see below, both in regards to previous accounts and my own analysis of the case, I believe that the case arguably represents one of the biggest pink herrings across Freud's work. My argument is that the focus on anal eroticism and the assumed corollary of latent homosexuality has limited much of what has since been made of the case, and indeed limited Freud's interpretation of the analytic material. In order to illustrate this claim, we can first turn to examine how previous writers have engaged with the case.

Previous accounts

As I noted above, much of what has previously been written about Freud's "From the history of an infantile neurosis" has taken as its coordinates Freud's own focus on homoeroticism, and specifically anal fixation. As we shall see below, in some instances this has involved an extension of Freud's arguments in terms of homoeroticism, whilst in other instances it has been to provide an alternate reading of (homo) sexuality in the case. Either way, I would suggest that a primary focus upon either homoeroticism or homosexuality elides some of the other interesting aspects of the case, a view that I share with Abraham and Torok (1986) whose excellent book on the case I discuss in some detail below. Before turning to examine this book, we can first look at the work of those authors who have centred homoeroticism and homosexuality in their discussions of the case.

In his discussion of whiteness and nationalism, López (2005, p. 163) suggests that the "homoerotic dimension of all the patient's father-surrogate object choices" is encapsulated in the binary of Germanic culture as masculine and Russian culture as feminine. Drawing attention to Sergei's German tutor, López suggests that the transference between Sergei and Freud was an "after affect" of the former's early affection for his tutor, an affection that López believes Freud failed to harness or acknowledge in terms of the apparent homoerotic nature of the transference and countertransference. Whilst the wider claims that López makes about the effects of whiteness and nationalism are useful, it would seem an overstatement to suggest that Freud did not acknowledge homoeroticism at work in the case. Indeed, it might be more productive to consider how Freud's own homosexual impulses shaped how he engaged with the transference.

The focus upon homoeroticism and homosexuality is also attended to by three writers who have closely examined what they view as anal eroticism evident in the case, and the ways in which it played out in the interchanges between Freud and Sergei. The first of these is Bersani (1995), whose work I referred to in the introduction to this book in regards to his discussion of receptive anal intercourse and the alleged crisis of masculinity that it evokes. In regards to Freud's "From the history of an infantile neurosis", Bersani suggests that the primal scene as supposedly witnessed by Sergei (one in which Freud suggests Sergei, at the age of eighteen months, witnessed his parents having intercourse *a tergo*) illustrates the homoeroticism at play in the analysis. Bersani suggests that Freud's emphasis on "discovering" the primal scene and thus accounting for Sergei's neurosis was driven as much by Sergei's anal eroticism as it was by Freud's own homoerotic desires. Despite this rather mundane focus on homoeroticism at the conscious interpersonal level, Bersani nonetheless makes an important contribution to our understanding of the case when he counters Freud's claim that in witnessing intercourse between his parents Sergei saw his mother as castrated. Instead, Bersani suggests that what Sergei witnessed was the castration of his father, whose penis Sergei allegedly saw "disappear" inside his mother during intercourse. This suggestion by Bersani is important in that it emphasises that heterosexual intercourse is not a union between an active and a passive party, nor is it a union between a castrated and an uncastrated party. Rather, as Bersani suggests, it is a site of loss—a loss we might suggest as pointing towards the failure of the sexual relationship to provide access to a fantasised sense of oneness formed by the union of a "matched pair".

Pursuing a somewhat different agenda in regards to homoeroticism in the case, Edelman (1991) suggests that the primal scene was a "sodomitical scene between sexually undifferentiated partners, both of whom, phantasmatically at least, are believed to possess the phallus" (p. 101). In one sense, Edeleman's argument has something useful to say about the sexual non-relationship (even if this was not explicitly his intent). Contrary to Bersani's (1995) argument (which implies that the infant Sergei could discern between his mother and his father in the sexual act), it can be inferred from Edelman's argument that the infant Sergei had not yet entered into language and hence had not experienced the castrating effects that this produces, thus he could view his parents as "undifferentiated partners". Importantly, however, whilst there is some utility in this argument, ultimately in many ways it is reliant upon the idea that we can know something of what came before the cut into language—that an analysis gives us access to an analysand's experience of life before the castrating effects of the entry into language.

Whilst Edelman does not explicitly make this argument about access to Sergei's infantile psychic life, it is an implication of his claim that in seeing both of his parents as in possession of the phallus, "it is small wonder that [Sergei had] little difficulty in experiencing an identification with each of their positions" (p. 101). This claim by Edelman is problematic, I would suggest, as it presumes that we can usefully know something about what an infant understands about the world around them prior to becoming a speakingbeing. My point here is not to deny that infants as biological beings understand the world around them. Rather, my point is that the kind of interpretation that Edelman makes (which presumes that an infant would see two parents as both possessing the phallus, and would interpret from this that they had access to each of their parent's positions) presupposes a speakingbeing. This presupposition is a result of Edelman conflating Freud's construction of the primal scene *a posteriori* with what Edelman treats as Sergei's apparent later desire to be "used from behind" by his father (p. 99). Such a conflation of events occurring at different registers, I would suggest, reflects Edelman's investment in emphasising anal sex as the issue at stake within the case.

In his book-length study of the case, Davis (1995) too has concerns about Edelman's (1991) account of the case. Davis suggests that

> [...] we must be cautious in identifying the way in which the "sodomitical" primal scene reconstructed by Freud does or does not evoke the "spectacle of gay male sex" [...]. The intercourse "from behind" [...] is not inherently an act of *anal* intercourse, even though later the little observer supposedly interpreted what he has seen according to just this theory—for obviously vaginal intercourse can occur "from behind". (pp. 149–150, original emphasis)

Davis raises this concern with Edelman's work on the basis of his supposition that the "little observer" could not have seen his parents as two undifferentiated individuals both in possession of the phallus. Davis suggests, instead, that witnessing the coitus *a tergo* meant that the young Sergei was able to differentiate between his parents not on the basis of their genitalia (Davis is clear that the differentiation he has in mind is not anatomical sex), but rather on the basis of their gender. What precisely Davis means by this is not entirely clear in his text, though it appears that he bases this claim on the sexual scenario in the presumed primal scene as one involving an "upright male" and a "bent-over female" (p. 152). It is these "body postures" that Davis sees as "gendering" the scene.

The account provide by Davis (1995), I would suggest, is as problematic as Edelman's (1991) outlined above. Edelman, as I suggested, claims that the infant Sergei saw his parents as undifferentiated, and then at a later date (after his entry into language it must be presumed) vacillated between identifying with his mother and father. This account, I believe, takes a supposed fantasy constructed after the event of the primal scene to account for the sexual non-relationship, and translates it to mean that Sergei acted as though he could occupy the position of both parents. In other words, Edeleman conflates fantasy with reality. Davis does the opposite: he appears to presume that the eighteen month old Sergei could perceive the "truth" of sexual difference, and from there could later experience both homosexual and heterosexual gratifications. For both Edelman and Davis, I would suggest, Sergei is seen as overcoming the sexual non-relationship in practice, rather than just in fantasy.

An entirely different account of the case is provided by Abraham and Torok (1986) in their beautifully written book on the case. Engaging in a close reading of the specific words used by Sergei and their differential meanings in English, German and Russian (the three languages he was exposed to from an early age), Abraham and Torok develop what they refer to as a "cryptonomy" of the case. In doing so, they take as their coordinates the fact that Sergei was seduced by his sister, and they suggest that she had also been intimate with their father. Abraham and Torok suggest that there were two competing positions that Sergei had incorporated and which are evidenced throughout the case material: that of the father and that of the sister.

In regards to his incorporation of his sister, Abraham and Torok (1986) suggest that this explains the homoeroticism evident in the case:

Has anyone seen a well-bred young man, not suspected of homosexuality, make such a request ["of performing anal coitus and an invitation to defecate on his head"] of an eminent specialist of fifty? No, really, he was no longer himself. (p. 23)

To interpolate my own framework in this book onto Abraham and Torok's suggestion, viewing Sergei's account of his early experiences and then his actions towards Freud as homoerotic or homosexual is thus a pink herring: it was his sister who held the sexualised viewpoint elaborated within the case, not *per se* the Sergei lying on the couch. Abraham and Torok substantiate this claim through a close reading of the dream of the wolves, which they suggest is a cryptonym for Sergei's desire for his sister to rub his penis. Their emphasis upon the role of the sister in Sergei's psychic life is one I will take up in my own analysis below.

Goodwin (2012) has subsequently taken up the framework provided by Abraham and Torok (1986), and in so doing has explored in greater detail the "cryptic dialogue of the bowel" that he believes is elided both by Freud, but also in Abraham and Torok's analysis. Instead of equating the "excretory function" (p. 5) of the bowels with anal eroticism, as Freud did, Goodwin suggests that the issue at stake for Sergei was not as simple as one of activity versus passivity. Rather, he suggests, what was at stake was more akin to the möbius strip, whether the boundary between inside and outside are blurred.

This point about activity and passivity being pink herrings in the case is furthered in a paper by Ferraro (2010), who suggests that whilst it may be true that Sergei treated passive and active as equitable to feminine and masculine, this was not Freud's argument at all. This equation appears, in differing ways, to have informed the arguments presented by Edelman (1991) and Davis (1995), where the logic of the fantasy that Sergei appeared to present is taken as a basis for a theory about homosexuality and heterosexuality, and masculinity and femininity. Ferraro's argument, I would suggest, does a better job of accounting for the sexual non-relationship. As I proposed above, both Edelman and Davis transpose Sergei's alleged fantasy (that functioned to discount the sexual non-relationship) onto his conscious actions and identifications. Ferraro, by contrast, maintains his focus on fantasy, in his suggestion that the fantasy of witnessing parental intercourse *a tergo* (if that is indeed what the fantasy was) functions to symbolise the sexual relationship in ways that create a union between man and woman. Different through similar to my focus below, this is a *fantasy* that attempts to account for the sexual non-relationship, which is wholly different to suggesting that Sergei consciously believed that he could position himself in such a way as to occupy both positions (his mother's and his father's) and thus deny the sexual non-relationship.

A focus on sexuation

As we shall now see in my analysis of the case, my interpretation of Sergei's position is that he represents the masculine side of the formula of sexuation *par excellence*. In my repeated reading of the case, in tandem with Abraham and Torok's (1986) reading, it became apparent to me that Sergei's position oscillates between the exception and the for-all. Rather than attempting to adjudicate as to which position best describes Sergei's location, in my analysis in this chapter I focus on both positions with reference to Sergei. After all, as we saw in chapter two, the masculine side of the equation is based upon an equivocation between the two masculine positions. In the other cases that I analyse in this book, those deciphered as being on the masculine side are typically more clearly located in one of the two masculine positions. Focusing on Sergei as equivocating between the two positions is useful both as it highlights the possibility that one position may not fully encapsulate a person's sexuation, and because it reminds us that the masculine side rests on an equivocation (unlike the feminine side, which involves a conditional relationship between the two positions).

Also unique to this case, at least as I interpret it, is my deciphering of Sergei's mother and father as both being in the position of the for-all. We shall return to this similarity in the final chapter to this book, to consider in further detail what this can tell us about the role of various positionings of parents in the neuroses of children. Finally in terms of positionings, my argument in this chapter, following Abraham and Torok (1986), is that Sergei deciphered his sister as being in the position of the exception. We can now turn to examine each of these positions in turn, starting with the sister.

I start with the sister, following Abraham and Torok (1986), as she appears to have been a lynchpin in the routing of Sergei's desire and thus his sexuation. As I noted earlier, Abraham and Torok take as central Freud's suggestion that the sister had seduced Sergei. Freud clearly reports this as follows:

> The patient suddenly called to mind the fact that, when he was still very small [...] his sister had seduced him into sexual practices. First came a recollection that in the lavatory, which the children used frequently to visit together, she had made this proposal: "Let's show our bottoms", and had proceeded from words to deeds. Subsequently the more essential part of the seduction came to light, with full particulars as to time and place. It was in spring, at a time when his father was away; the children were in one room playing on the floor, while their mother was working in the next. His sister had taken hold of his penis and played with it. (p. 20)

His sister was a person, then, for whom the incest taboo did not operate, and further who was to a certain degree beyond the rules of the parents: she could seduce Sergei with their mother just next door, and when their father was away and thus powerless to intervene. Whilst only being two years older than Sergei, this was nonetheless a person with considerable power over him and indeed those around her. In his account of the case, Freud then goes on to state that Sergei was not equally able to exert power over his sister in later years:

> During the tempestuous sexual excitement of his puberty he ventured upon an attempt at an intimate physical approach [to his sister]. She rejected him with equal decision and dexterity, and he at once turned away from her to a little peasant girl who was a servant in the house and had the same name as his sister. In doing so he was taking a step which had a determinant influence on his heterosexual choice of object, for all the girls with whom he subsequently fell in love—often with the clearest indications of compulsion—were also servants, whose education and intelligence were necessarily far inferior to his own. If all of these objects of his love were substitutes for the figure of the sister whom he had to forgo, then it could not be denied that an intention of debasing his sister and of putting an end to her intellectual superiority, which he had formerly found so oppressive, had obtained the decisive control over his object-choice. (p. 22)

These claims by Freud are central to my analysis of the case in terms of suggesting both that the sister was deciphered by Sergei as being in the position of the exception, and that Sergei chose a position that was an equivocation between the exception and the for-all. Clearly, given the rejection by his sister, Sergei could not be located solely in the position of the exception: He could be had by his sister, but he could not in turn have his sister. So instead he did the next best thing: he turned his attractions to vulnerable young women who served as substitutes for his sister. In this way, I would argue, he could have his sister. I would differ from Freud in my interpretation, however, in that I don't think *per se* that it was Sergei's intention to debase his sister by taking up with peasant girls and servants. I do think, nonetheless, that taking up with such women allowed him to both remain the for-all who was the recipient of his sister's seduction, but to at the same time seduce young women who functioned as versions of his sister, and in so doing to occupy the position of the exception. This, then, is the equivocation mentioned above: he was the for-all who existed in a relationship to an exception (his sister), and at the same time in his fantasy he was also the exception who could have the peasant girl and the servants, who functioned as proxies for his sister.

As I noted earlier, Abraham and Torok (1986) suggest that the dream of the wolves was about the sister, not the father. I will make the perhaps surprising move of not repeating the dream here, as I don't feel that it has anything additional to offer in terms of the position of the sister and Sergei as outlined above. What I will now examine, however, are the associations that Sergei reported to Freud in terms of the wolves that he saw sitting in a tree outside his bedroom window in the dream:

> How did the wolves come to be on the tree? This reminded him of a story that he had heard his grandfather tell [...]. A tailor was sitting at work in his room, when the window opened and a wolf leapt in. The tailor hit after him with his yard—no (he corrected himself), caught him by his tail and pulled it off, so that the wolf ran away in terror. Some time later the tailor went into the forest, and suddenly saw a pack of wolves coming towards him; so he climbed up a tree to escape from them. At first the wolves were in perplexity; but the maimed one, which was among them and wanted to revenge himself on the tailor, proposed that they should climb one upon another till the last one could reach him. He himself—he was a vigorous old

fellow—would be the base of the pyramid. The wolves did as he suggested, but the tailor had recognised the visitor whom he had punished, and suddenly called out as he had before: "Catch the grey one by his tail!" The tailless wolf, terrified by the recollection, ran away, and all the others tumbled down. (p. 31)

Perhaps obviously, my suggestion is that in these associations the sister is the tailor and the father is the old grey wolf. Whilst, as I noted above, Abraham and Torok (1986) associate the wolf dream with the sister, it is not *per se* the wolves that represent the sister. Rather, it is the number of wolves and their positioning within the tree. As Abraham and Torok note, and drawing on their translations from Russian dialect, six wolves are a sixster of wolves—a sister. The wolves in the dream are thus not a literal representation of the sister, but rather she appears as the very syntax of the dream. How then do we understand the father as the wolf in the association to the dream?

First, we must note that the associations reported by Sergei above are derived from his grandfather's story. Specifically, this was Sergei's mother's father. In the case notes we are told by Freud that Sergei's Nanya [his old Russian nanny] "told him that his sister was his mother's child, but that he was his father's" (p. 17). If the sister is the mother's child, I would suggest then that the sister is also the grandfather's grandchild. As a result, we can see that the sister is again inserted into the syntax of the story, through the role of the protagonist (i.e., it is the grandfather telling about his granddaughter's exploits, according to Sergei's interpretation). With this in mind, it is relatively easy to see how the roles of the sister and father are made intelligible by the associations to the dream. The tailor was in the position of someone who could not be had—the wolf twice attempted to get the tailor (when he jumped through the window, and then when he tried to reach the tailor in the tree), but on both occasions the tailor was unreachable. This is reminiscent of the story above of Sergei attempting to proposition his sister and failing, but also of his father's lack of authority over the sister.

The association also gives some merit to the argument by Abraham and Torok (1986) that the sister at some point seduced the father. In the association the tailor "pulls off" the tail of the fox who is left terrorised, and who is latter terrified when forced to recollect the experience of having his tail pulled off. The actions of the tailor/sister are important here, as they again position her in the place of the exception who can have the father/wolf, despite the incest taboo. Importantly, this having ("pulling") is different to the position of the father, who is had ("pulled"). Despite his potentially incestuous interactions with his daughter, he is not in the position of the exception as it is he who is had. Of course my claim here is not that he was without agency and thus a victim—he was after all a father, and she a child. Furthermore, we do not know if this sexual intimacy actually occurred between the father and sister. What we do know, at least as far as my argument stands, is that Sergei deciphered his sister as being in the position of one who has, and his father in the position of one who is had.

This then brings us to the position of the father. It would be too simple, as at times Freud does, to interpret the father as being in the position of the exception. Freud tells us that the father came to prefer the sister over Sergei, and that Sergei felt a considerable amount of fear of his father. But these are all rather obvious and conscious associations. There are other, unconscious, associations to the father that perhaps suggest more correctly that Sergei deciphered him as in the position of the for-all—as one who had access only to a limited form of phallic jouissance—he could not have every person he desired, only some. A key example of this appears in Freud's account of Sergei's compulsion to breathe out when he saw cripples and beggars. Towards the end of his presentation of the case Freud suggests that Sergei's

> Father was thus the prototype of all the cripples, beggars, and poor people in whose presence he was obliged to breathe out; just as a father is the prototype of the bogies that people see in anxiety-states, and of the caricatures that are drawn to bring derision upon some one. (p. 67)

The father is thus viewed by Sergei as being in the position of the pitiful beggar, the one who could be had by the sister, the one whose tail could be pulled. This is a person who is a recipient of other people's commands. As we can see in the following recollection, the mother too is positioned as the for-all, however this takes a different form to the position of the father as for-all:

> One day there emerged, timidly and indistinctly, a kind of recollection that at a very early age, even before the time of the nurse, he must have had a nursery-maid who was very fond of him. Her name had been the same as his mother's. He had no doubt returned

her affection. It was, in fact, a first love that had faded into oblivion
[…]. Then on another occasion he amended this recollection. She
could not have had the same name as his mother; that had been a
mistake on his part, and it showed, of course, that in his memory
she had become fused with his mother. (p. 90)

Whilst through her fusion with the position of the nursery-maid the
mother appears to be deciphered by Sergei as the for-all, there is nonetheless a fondness expressed with reference to the mother via her association with the nursery-maid. Abraham and Torok (1986) note that
Sergei experienced a caring relationship with his mother, which is
unsurprising given they were both located to a certain degree on the
outer with reference to the presumed relationship between the father
and sister.

This claim about the relationship between Sergei and his mother is
important in the context of his sexuation. As I have argued above, the
father appears to have enacted an ineffectual "no" for both his son and
daughter. This might lead us to question whether Sergei had a psychotic
structure, as Davis (1995) suggests. Yet as I noted in the introduction to
this chapter with regards to the broad contours of the case, Sergei experienced a "no" in the form of religious beliefs, which importantly were
introduced to him by his mother. Also as I noted above, his sister was
in the position of the exception, and as Freud notes "played an important part in his life" (p. 14), though this does not mean she stood in for
either Sergei's first or second Other. Rather, she played a rather unique
role in determining how Sergei viewed his first and second Other, one
that requires a qualification to my suggestion in chapter two that the
latter plays a significant role in determining the position of the former.
In Freud's "From the history of an infantile neurosis" it would appear
that it was the sister who most clearly shaped how Sergei deciphered
the position of his first Other. My suggestion is not that the father was
entirely redundant, but rather that whilst religious beliefs potentially
performed the role of the "no" of the father, Sergei came to decipher
the position of his mother not primarily through religion, but through
his sister.

This is perhaps clearest in the following dream that Sergei reported
to Freud:

"I had a dream," he said, "of a man tearing off the wings of an
Espe." "*Espe*?" I asked; "what do you mean by that?" "You know;

that insect with yellow stripes on its body, that stings." This must be an allusion to Grusha, the pear with the yellow stripes. I could now put him right: "So what you mean is a *Wespe* [wasp]." "Is it called a *Wespe*? I really thought it was called an *Espe*." (Like so many other people, he used his difficulties with a foreign language as a screen for symptomatic acts.) "But *Espe*, why, that's myself: S. P." (which were his initials). The *Espe* was of course a mutilated *Wespe*. (p. 94)

In order to understand this dream, we must note that Grusha was the name of the aforementioned nursery-maid whom Sergei had fused in his memory with his mother, and "grusha" was also the word for "pear" in Russian, which Sergei associated with a particular type of pear that had yellow stripes on it. This dream is important, then, as not only does the wasp represent the mother and the peasant girls/servants to whom Sergei was attracted to in lieu of his sister, but it also represents Sergei himself (as he notes in his misunderstanding of the word "*wespe*"). This again suggests that both Sergei and his mother were in similar positions in relation to the one (i.e., the sister, the tail puller) who tears off the wings.

Very importantly here, however, there is an important caveat to the story of the wasp who has its wings pulled off. On one level, as I noted above, the dream alludes to the position of the sister as the exception, and to Sergei and his mother as located within the position of the for-all. Yet at the same time, we are talking here about a wasp "*that stings*" (my emphasis). This stinging function is important with reference to both Sergei and his mother: they have some sting left in them, despite their wings being pulled off. Importantly, however, I would not go so far as to suggest that the wasp represents someone who has access to an other form of jouissance (i.e., they are not located in either of the positions on the feminine side of the formulate of sexuation). Instead, for Sergei as he is represented within the dream, this is again someone whose sexuation rests on the equivocation between the exception and the for-all. I have already demonstrated this above in regards to Sergei, but here I would suggest that the same may also have been true for the mother, though I can give no further evidence to support this claim from the case, and hence do not go so far as to accord her a position of equivocation, instead remaining with my suggestion above that Sergei deciphered his mother as being in the position of the for-all.

So what does all of this tell us about the fantasy in which Sergei's desire circulated, and through which he was able to account for the sexual non-relationship? The fantasy, as I have already alluded to above, is one in which he is both had and has: in which he is both the for-all and the exception. This account of the fantasy perhaps explains why writers such as Edelman (1991) and Davis (1995) have produced accounts of the case in which they attempt to position Sergei as being both masculine and feminine, both homosexual and heterosexual. This, I have suggested, is a pink herring, but it is nonetheless of a kind with what I am suggesting, namely that there is an equivocation going on, though not necessarily one related to object choice or identification, but rather one related to sexuation. In his fantasy Sergei could both have his sister (and by extrapolation through the having of the peasant girl and servants associated first with his sister and then his mother, have his mother), and also be had by his sister (and as a result be like his father). This, then, is a fantasy of overcoming the sexual non-relationship by being able to shift positions and thus maintain the fantasy of two positions coming together in a union as one. Different to Edelman and Davis, however, my suggestion is not necessarily that this is what Sergei consciously sought to achieve.

In terms of the object a, this is somewhat difficult to pinpoint in this case, primarily because of the complex relationship between the sister, the mother, and the father. Whilst, as I argued above, the mother is in the position of the first Other, the failure of the "no" of the father himself, and the role of religious piety standing in for the "no", makes it somewhat more difficult to identify the little piece of jouissance that Sergei held onto within his fantasy as a way of accessing a sense of oneness with his first Other. I would suggest that the dream of the wasp is the closest we have to coordinates for Sergei's object a. As I established above, as the wasp he is both the one whose wings are removed, but also the one who can sting. This is a position that rests upon the equivocation that structures the masculine side of the formula of sexuation. Yet there is more to be taken from this dream. What falls to the wayside in the act of tearing? Is it the wings or the yellow striped body? Given the association of the wasp to the pear (grusha) to the nursery-maid (Grusha) to the mother, what remains at the end is the mutilated body, and what falls to the wayside are the wings. The wings, I would suggest, represent the object a.

In the structure of this particular dream, if the little piece of jouissance is represented by the wings, we can conjecture that the fantasy of equivocation rests not simply on shifting positions and thus creating a union, but that it is *through* Sergei that the sexual non-relationship may be overcome: it is he who can reinstate his mother's wings. Evidence is given for this conjecture from a memory provided to Freud by Sergei:

> He was chasing a beautiful big butterfly with yellow stripes and large wings which ended in pointed projections—a swallow-tail, in fact. Suddenly, when the butterfly had settled on a flower, he was seized with a dreadful fear of the creature, and ran away screaming […]. He added that in general butterflies had seemed to him like women and girls, and beetles and caterpillars like boys. So there could be little doubt that in this anxiety scene a recollection of some female person had been aroused. (p. 89)

In this memory, then, the wings very much seem to stand in for a female person as Freud notes, my suggestion being that they stood in for his mother. The fact that his proximity to the wings produced such anxiety in this memory suggests to me that we are indeed onto something in suggesting that the wings represent the object *a* in the fantasy, for as Lacan (2014) noted, we experience anxiety precisely when we are too close to our object *a*. We might further ask what does a wasp without its wings look like, if not something more like a beetle or a caterpillar? This affirms my supposition that it is Sergei who, in his fantasy, could give his mother back her wings, and in so doing affirm the "correct-ness" of her position as a woman (and his position and that of his father as men), again indicating that the fantasy and the object *a* within it was centrally about overcoming the sexual non-relationship. And again, of a kind with Edelman (1991) and Davis (1995), the logic that Sergei's dream and memories provide are a fantasy about the interchangeability of women and men (i.e., wings or no-wings), but importantly this was a fantasy, not *per se* a conscious reality.

Conclusions

In my analysis of Freud's "From the history of an infantile neurosis" I have demonstrated how the position of Sergei can only be understood via a complex set of coordinates that have previously been read as centring masculinity/femininity and homosexuality/heterosexuality. These readings, I have suggested, are pink herrings in that they are reliant to a certain degree upon the interpretation of particular actions or identifications as a truth about Sergei's conscious self. By contrast, in this chapter I have suggested that the fantasy through which the equivocation between the exception and for-all played out for Sergei—and the object *a* within the fantasy—indicate an alternate way of understanding Sergei's complex sexuated positioning in relation to his mother, father, and sister.

Also of importance in this chapter has been my discussion of the role of religion as the "no" of the father, and what this meant in terms of how Sergei was left to try and negotiate the powerful role of his sister, his close relationship with his mother (in terms of positioning), and how the latter differed in fantasy to the father, even if the positions they were deciphered as being in were the same. This difference in sameness is a point I will return to in the final chapter of this book, where I explore its implications for how we may ensure that any clinical focus on sexuation does not slip into a search for difference or sameness.

CHAPTER FOUR

Fragment of an analysis of a case of hysteria

The case

Of all of Freud's cases, arguably the most has been written about his "Fragment of an analysis of a case of hysteria" (1905e). The volume of writing about this case is at least in part a product of feminist critiques and engagements with Freudian psychoanalysis, with the case often taken as evidence of the sexism inherent to Freud's work. As with all of Freud's cases, multiple readings are possible. In this chapter (as with all of the analytic chapters in this book) my focus is not *per se* to engage with critiques of Freud's work, though at the same time my intent is not to remain politically unengaged from previous accounts of the case. Remaining focused on sexuation, I would suggest, is not apolitical. Rather, as this chapter will demonstrate, there is a politics attached to a reading of sexuation, one that I will touch on briefly as I present my analysis, and one that I will explore in further detail in the final chapter of this book.

Turning to the case itself, a second reason why so much has been written about it is that perhaps of all of Freud's cases, it is the one with the most twists and turns in terms of his analytic exposition of the case materials. Whilst certainly Freud's other cases similarly involve twists and turns—something to be expected given the metaleptic nature of analytic practice—in his "Fragment of an analysis of a case of hysteria" the twists and turns arguably represent Freud's own processes of establishing and clarifying the analytic technique, and further honing his approach to the analysis of dreams. Also contributing to the twists and turns of the case are the operations of transference and countertransference, operations that Freud was only just in the process of understanding and theorising when he conducted the analysis.

Having provided these brief notes on the wider setting of the case and responses to it, we can now turn to the case itself. As is true of previous chapters in this book, my interest is not to provide an overview of Freud's analysis of the case. Rather, my focus is on what I perceive to be the key narrative of the case as told by the analysand, Dora. Dora, of course, was the pseudonym that Freud gave to his patient Ida Bauer. Mahoney (1996) discusses in some detail the possible meanings associated with the pseudonym that Freud chose. For the purposes of this chapter (and unlike most of the other chapters in this book) I will retain the pseudonym of Dora, partly because the case it so well known as the "Dora case", and partly because, unlike in most of Freud's other cases, an actual pseudonym was used (as compared to, for example, "the homosexual woman" or the "Rat man").

So what do we know of Dora as Freud tells it? From her childhood, we are told, Dora had suffered from a range of illnesses. Various doctors, including Freud, had viewed the majority of these illnesses as hysterical formations, though some were also seen as having an organic basis. Dora's father, too, had experienced many bouts of significant illness, necessitating the family relocating at varying times of the year to a health resort. Dora had often taken on a significant role in caring for her father during his illnesses. To a large degree, Freud ties the father's illnesses to a case of syphilis prior to his marriage to Dora's mother, and conjectures at varying points throughout the case as to whether the disease had played a significant role in Dora's own illnesses.

In terms of Dora's mother and father, with regard to the former, Freud has relatively little to say, characterising her as a person displaying "housewife's psychosis" (p. 20), referring specifically to her obsessions related to house cleaning and orderliness. Illnesses aside, Dora's father is presented by Freud as an accomplished businessman, well regarded in his community. Freud characterises the marriage as an unhappy one, and indeed much of the case focuses on the outcomes of this unhappiness.

Specifically in regards to the parents' unhappiness, much emphasis is placed in Freud's account upon the relationship between Dora's father and a family friend: a woman—whom Freud refers to as Frau K.—who holidayed with Dora's family, and with whom Dora's entire family were well acquainted. Dora believed that her father and this woman were having an affair, one consequence of which being that the woman's husband—Herr K.—turned his attention to Dora. We are told of two particular instances where Herr K. had made advances upon Dora. In the first, when Dora was fourteen, he had arranged it so that he and Dora were alone in his shop, at which time he pressed himself up against her and kissed her. Dora reported a feeling of disgust arising from this event, one that Freud argued generalised to other men. The second advance occurred several years later, when Dora and Herr K. were walking together near a lake. During this walk Herr K. attempted to convey to Dora his feelings for her, but Dora cut him off with a slap to his face, and walked away from the situation. As we will see below, this slap, I argue, offers much analytic insight in terms of sexuation.

These advances made by Herr K. led to Dora insisting to her father that the family break off contact with the K's. This, of course, was not appealing to Dora's father, who whilst sympathetic towards his daughter, did not want to prevent a continued relationship with Frau K. As a result, both Dora's father and Herr K. argued that Dora's claims about the advances made by Herr K. were fictions created Dora. This denial led to considerable and understandable anger on Dora's behalf, and soured her relationship with her father (which previously had been positive, in comparison to her relationship with her mother, which had never been particularly positive).

Dora's parents brought her to see Freud due to concerns over a note they had found in her desk, which indicated that she intended to take her life. Dora had previously experienced "low spirits", "fatigue and a lack of concentration" (p. 23), all of which were in addition to her physical illnesses. By the conclusion of her relatively brief analysis (Dora broke the analysis off after only three months), Freud suggests that some of her symptoms had abated, though certainly she was far from being "cured".

I will introduce some further details about the case below (including the two dreams that Freud analyses), but for now this brief description of the key aspects of Dora's life as reported by Freud serves to provide enough of an overview for the reader so that the following summary of some of the key previous accounts of the case is intelligible.

Previous accounts

Hopefully without doing a disservice to previous account of Freud's "Fragment of an analysis of a case of hysteria", in this section I first present accounts that may be broadly classified as Freudian, before then presenting accounts that may be broadly classified as Lacanian. In creating these two groupings my aim is not to insist that the authors themselves identify as either Freudians or Lacanians (though some do), but rather to indicate that the first set of accounts largely take as their theoretical framework that provided by Freud, whereas the second set are oriented by Lacan's reworkings of Freud, specifically with reference to the Dora case.

In regards to those that I am classifying as Freudian, there is a general agreement that by Freud's account Dora displayed a masculine identification. The rationale for making such a claim, however, is diverse, drawing on differing aspects of the case to justify an interpretation of Dora as identified with either her father or brother, and that this identification "led" to her attraction to, and desire for, Frau K. It is important for me to say at the outset that I believe that this interpretation is a significant pink herring. Freud voices this pink herring explicitly, where he notes in a footnote to the postscript of the case that:

> The longer the interval of time that separates me from the end of this analysis, the more probable it seems to me that the fault in my technique lay in this omission: I failed to discover in time and to inform the patient that her homosexual (gynaecophilic) love for Frau K. was the strongest unconscious current in her mental life. (p. 120)

The question of whether Dora displayed a masculine identification aside (a question I will unpack in detail in a moment), what perhaps concerns me the most is that even if Dora had a masculine identification, why should this automatically mean that she was attracted to women? Such an account, of course, is entirely different to the account of sexuation I have developed in this book—that is obvious. But even beyond that difference, I would suggest that there is an inherent problem in equating identification—however it is formulated—as automatically leading to a particular object choice. Perhaps in the case of Freud he is owed some empathy, given that the dominant understanding of the time would indeed have emphasised the idea that masculinity and femininity are opposites. Yet I would suggest that it is precisely this understanding that introduces all sorts of problems into any analysis of the case if it is presumed that a particular identification must automatically lead to a particular object choice. As I argued in chapter two, what this ignores is the *position* of the person in whom the object *a* is located. In other words, reducing identification and object choice to assigned sex only takes us a very limited way down the path of understanding desire.

Having stated these concerns about the limitations of any assumption about "opposites", and the fact this constitutes a pink herring, let us now look more closely at what has been said about Dora's identification, firstly in terms of what has been read as her masculine identification.

Perhaps the most well-known collection of accounts of Freud's "Fragment of an analysis of a case of hysteria" appears in the edited collection *In Dora's Case* (Bernheimer & Kahane, 1985). Several of the authors whose accounts appear in this collection classify Dora as having a masculine identification. Hertz (1985), for example, emphasises Freud's use of the masculine pronoun when accounting for how Dora came to acquire knowledge of a sexual nature. In accepting Freud's account as positioning knowledge gained from reading books as masculine, Hertz then suggests that what Freud reads as Dora's dream about female genitals "is bound to be from the man's point of view" (p. 236). My first concern with the logic presented by Hertz is that it takes Freud's use of a masculine pronoun ("Anyone who employed such names […] must have derived his knowledge from books") as saying something about Dora. We could just as easily note that throughout Freud's work he uses the pronoun "he" to refer to all people when speaking in the abstract, as was characteristic of the time.

My second concern with Hertz' (1985) work pertains to the pink herring I outlined above: Dora having a dream about female genitals (if this was indeed the case) is in no way "bound" to a particular identification on Dora's behalf. A dream that is read as denoting an interest in female genitalia could be about Dora herself, just as easily as it could be about Dora's attraction to a woman as a feminine identified person.

The binding of identification to attraction in this way provides a rather simplistic account of sexuation, fantasy and desire, and indeed is not one that Freud himself entirely seemed to follow (despite the footnote mentioned above).

Rose (1985), also in the collection *In Dora's Case* (Bernheimer & Kahane, 1985), also suggests that Dora displayed a masculine identification, although Rose makes this claim from a different starting point within the case. Rose states that Dora's symptom—her cough—mirrored the cough that her father had. Rose also notes that some of Dora's memories about her relationship with her brother demonstrate her masculine identification. Rose also suggests that Dora identified with a man—a potential suitor—in her second dream.

Like Hertz (1985), Rose (1985) makes the leap that a masculine identification explains Dora's attraction to women, specifically to Frau K. Rose complicates this claim by suggesting that the "'true object of Dora's jealousy (made clear for no other reason by the over insistence of her reproaches against her father) [was] Frau K." (p. 133). This assumption that a masculine identification "explains" attraction to a woman is problematic, as outlined above. Rose's statement is also problematic for its use of the word jealous. Jealousy is typically understood as involving three parties: the person, the person they fear losing, and the person who may take them away. Is Rose suggesting that the father was going to take Frau K. away? This does not entirely ring true given the fact that, if anything, were Dora to have the alleged object of her affection she would be taking her (Frau K.) away from her father. Rose's claim makes somewhat more sense if we substitute the word "envy" for "jealousy", as envy involves only two parties: a person who wants something, and a person (or object) that is wanted. From this we could say that the true object of Dora's envy was Frau K., though this still doesn't "prove" a masculine identification.

The problems with Rose's (1985) account above are compounded later in her chapter, where she appears to argue that Dora's masculine identification is a problem for Dora, in that whilst it allows her access to the maternal body, it also "threatens the very category of identification itself" (p. 137). By my interpretation, Rose appears to be suggesting here that as someone assigned female at birth, Dora's alleged masculine identification is a problem as it doesn't "align" correctly with her assigned sex. Rose doesn't state this explicitly, but certainly implies it by suggesting that in her desire for Frau K. Dora can never "be placed as a 'true' feminine". Here Rose seems to insist that Dora's alleged masculine identification is in conflict with the truth of her as a person assigned female.

Whilst my reading of Rose (1985) is partial, it is driven in part by her role as a translator of Lacan's *Seminar XX* in which he explicated the formula of sexuation. Whilst this might suggest that I should not be summarising Rose's chapter under the banner of "Freudian", there is very little about her chapter that suggests a Lacanian reading. Indeed, in the section of the chapter described in the paragraph above Rose makes the claim that Dora's masculine identification is a threat to Dora as it suggests that the "category of sexual difference is not established" (p. 137). This to me would seem to assume that there is a veridical interpretation of sexual difference possible, and that had it been established Dora might have "properly" located herself on the side of the feminine. Such an account ignores Lacan's discussion of the sexual non-relationship and treats "sexual difference" as a "natural" reflection of assigned sex. It is for these reasons that I both dissent from Rose's reading, and locate her account within a Freudian framework.

The final chapter from *In Dora's Case* (Bernheimer & Kahane, 1985) that I summarise here is by Gallop (1985), who provides perhaps the most nuanced account of the three that I include here. Gallop does not so easily accept the according of a masculine identification to Dora, and instead explores how Dora positions herself in a relationship to Freud. Gallop specifically takes up the moment when Dora announced that she was terminating the analysis. Freud asked Dora when she made this decision, to which she replied "a fortnight ago". Freud tells her "That sounds just like a maidservant or a governess—a fortnight's warning" (1905e, p. 105). From this, Gallop asks the question of whether in making her statement "a fortnight ago" Dora was positioning herself as the maidservant giving her notice, or the employer giving the maidservant her notice. Gallop eventually settles on the interpretation that Freud was positioned as the one being given their notice, though Gallop rightly hesitates in allocating to Dora a masculine position (though she does allocate to Freud a feminine position). Whilst very different to the analysis I provide below, Gallop's interpretation of the case is nonetheless of a kind in that it recognises that understanding Dora's position requires understanding the position of those around her—how the way she deciphers their position tells us something about her own position.

Moving on from the chapters in *In Dora's Case* (Bernheimer & Kahane, 1985), arguably the most detailed examination of "Fragment of an analysis of a case of hysteria" is provided by Mahoney (1996) in his book-length examination of the case. Mahoney's text has much to recommend it, specifically his in-depth explication of the family history and his clarification of key issues that are elided in the case. Mahoney also provides alternate translations of the two dreams that are analysed in the case, and I will use these translations in my analysis below. At the same time, however, Mahoney is strident in his view that Dora was abused by both her father and by Herr K., and that Freud perpetuated this abuse. Rather oddly, Mahoney's is not a feminist critique of the abuse of women by men (odd in the sense that there is a considerable amount of feminist writing on the Dora case that discusses abuse), and in my reading Mahoney's view is perhaps rather over determined: In reading the case I do not see abuse in quite the places or ways that Mahoney does.

These caveats about Mahoney's (1996) book aside, it has much to offer us in terms of a Freudian account of identification in the case. Specifically, Mahoney affirms Freud's supposition that he had failed to adequately attend to Dora's homosexual desires, though importantly Mahoney does not assume that if Dora desired Frau K., it was automatically from a masculine identification. Dissenting from Gallop's (1985) account outlined above, Mahoney locates Freud in a masculine position, and suggests that, at least early in the case, Dora was identified with her mother. This supposition on Mahoney's part is important in as it leaves open a space for one woman to love another from a feminine position, an important space as outlined by Hamer (1990) in regards to Freud's (1920a) "The psychogenesis of a case of homosexuality in a woman" as discussed in chapter three.

Despite having opened this space, however, upon analysing the second dream in the case Mahoney (1996) affirms the writers above who have viewed Dora as occupying a masculine position. Mahoney, at least in part, makes this claim on the basis of the fact that at the time of the analysis, in Vienna Dora's last name (Bauer) "was slang for 'sperm'" (p. 92). Whilst this is certainly an interesting observation, it again offers a rather simplistic account of identification by relying upon the masculinisation of sperm and its meaning to Dora.

Turning to Lacanian accounts of the case, Adams (1996) provides an account of identification that is productive in the sense that it critiques the assumption that Freud appears to make (and as discussed above in regards to Freudian accounts of the case), namely that identifications are formed in terms of opposites. Also important for the analysis I present below, Adams suggests that:

> It seems that it is important to specify the underlying fantasy because it concerns Dora's sexual position; that is, she takes up a masculine position if she identifies with her father, a feminine one if she identities with Frau K. But is this the case? Once Dora identifies with one, does she not also identify with the other? For fantasy is laid out in scenarios and the subject can take up now one position, now another in the scenario. (p. 13)

Adams, however, focuses specifically on whether Dora was "active" or "passive" in her fantasy, thus making an argument entirely different to the one I make in the analysis below.

Unlike Adams (1996), but like the majority of the Freudian accounts outlined above, Van Haute and Geyskens (2012), in a chapter that employs a Lacanian account of the case, argue that *because* Dora was attracted to Frau K., she identified with Herr K. Their argument rests on the supposition that homosexual desire wasn't viable for Dora, so she needed to adopt a masculine identification so as to avoid homosexuality. Whilst, like Rose (1985) above, it could be suggested that there is nothing about this account that is Lacanian, I include it here along with other Lacanian accounts due to the fact that Van Haute and Geyskens position their chapter as being Lacanian (which Rose does not do).

In terms of the slap that Dora gave to Herr K. by the lake, Ragland (2006a; 2006b) and Gherovici (2010) give two differing accounts of this event in terms of sexuation and identification. Ragland suggests that Dora identified with Frau K., and that when in his proposition to her Herr K. told Dora that he got nothing from his wife, this served to position Dora as an object, hence the slap. In a similar way, Ragland suggests that when Freud insisted upon naming masturbation and a love for Herr K. as Dora's secret desire, she was denied a subjective position within her fantasy, hence the termination of the analysis.

Gherovici's (2010) account of the slap, by contrast, is the closest to the one I will outline in my analysis below. Gherovici suggests that the slap was the product of a "charge of anxiety" brought about by an "encounter not filtered by desire and deprived of the veil of fantasy".

Gherovici suggests that Herr K's statement about his wife broke Dora's identification with Frau K., and hence she was "confronted with the enigma of sex with nothing to safeguard her" (p. 118). Gherovici also suggests that Freud similarly broke down the veil of fantasy by insisting upon Herr K. as the real object of Dora's desire, rather than as someone a part of whom possibly represented Dora's object *a*. As we shall now see, Gherovici's argument about the circulation of desire and the role of the object *a* touches upon the claims about sexuation that I make in regards to the case.

A focus on sexuation

As I noted above, a particular hallmark of Freud's "Fragment of an analysis of a case of hysteria" are the twists and turns in the account that he provides. So twisted is it that the reader can be left wondering who exactly the chief protagonists are. This is a matter of some import, given the fact that what we are looking for when we are considering sexuation are the positions deciphered by the analysand in regards to their first and second Other, and what that can tell us about their own position. Certainly in his report of the case, Freud is largely dismissive of the role of Dora's mother, instead emphasising the central role of Dora's father to her psychical life. It could be tempting to thus read Dora's father as her first Other, and her mother (or someone else altogether) as Dora's second Other. This, however, I think would be an error. We are given very little information in the case about Dora's early life, and thus it would seem unwise to accept Freud's determination that Dora's mother played no significant role in her life. Furthermore, whilst we are told that Dora and her brother had a governess to care for them, this would have been typical of a family such as theirs at the time, and again no warrant to presume that Dora's mother did not function as her first Other. As such, it seems appropriate to look to Dora's mother as her first Other, and as we shall see below, this seems warranted by at least one (if not both) of the dreams reported in the case.

As I noted earlier, in the analysis I present here I utilise Mahoney's (1996) translation of the two dreams. Below I provide first Strachey's translation and then Mahoney's:

> A house was on fire. My father was standing beside my bed and
> woke me up. I dressed quickly. Mother wanted to stop and save

her jewel-case; but Father said: "I refuse to let myself and my two children be burnt for the sake of your jewel-case." We hurried downstairs, and as soon as I was outside I woke up. (p. 64)

It's burning in a house, Dora recounted; Father is standing before my bed and wakes me up. I dress myself quickly. Mama, though, wants to save her jewel box, but Papa says: "I don't want myself and both my children to be burnt up by fire because of your jewel box." We hurry downstairs, and as soon as I am outside, I wake up. (p. 77)

As we can see by comparing the two translations (and as Mahoney notes), the differences are important. In Strachey's translation the past tense is used. In Mahoney's translation the present tense is used. Other notable differences are that in Strachey's translation states a house was on fire (i.e., all of it), whilst Mahoney's translation suggests that there is burning *in* a house. These differences noted, let us now turn to first look at the position of Dora's mother within the dream.

In his explication of the case, Freud emphasises a depiction of Dora's mother within the dream as selfish—what mother would sacrifice her children for a jewel box? But this is a moral question imposed on a dream. A more useful question to ask, I would suggest, is why a jewel box was seen by Dora as being so important to her mother? In other words, rather than accepting the contrast between what Freud implicitly treats as "your money or your (children's) life", we might more productively consider why in the dream Dora saw her mother as focused on the jewel box to the exclusion of everything else.

In his *Seminar XI*, Lacan (1977) suggested that the opposition between "your money or your life" is illusory. Lacan suggested that if you choose your money, then you lose your life. But a life without money isn't much of a life at all. What, then, would life without the jewel box have meant for Dora's mother in the dream? This question leads me to suggest that Dora deciphered her mother as being in the position of the no exception. This was a person located on the feminine side of the formula of sexuation, a speakingbeing who, it appeared to Dora, wanted or had access to some form of jouissance beyond the phallic, yet what it was that she wanted was unclear or known, perhaps even to Dora's mother. As such, and despite Freud's considerable emphasis upon the jewel box in his explication of the case, the jewel box itself is something of a pink herring: it isn't necessarily, as Freud tells us, all about female genitalia. It doesn't necessarily tell us, as Mahoney (1996) would have it, that Dora was dreaming of "masturbating [Frau K.] or someone else, perhaps even *inside* of her own vagina" (p. 80).

In contrast to these types of interpretations of the jewel box in the dream, I would suggest that the jewel box thus tells us more about how Dora deciphered the position of her mother than it tells us about Dora's own position (though of course, as we shall see, the two are intimately related). As I indicated above, why else would Dora's mother in the dream risk her own life and her children's unless the jewel box represented something that she desired. My point here is not that the jewel box itself is the "truth" of Dora's mother's desire. It is simply a marker within the dream that her mother had a desire, and one that is located perhaps beyond phallic jouissance: a mother who might choose a jewel box over herself or her children is not a mother by phallic standards. Instead, she is something else, something more, whilst that something remains elusive.

Beyond the dream, there are further examples of the elusive nature of Dora's mother's desire, despite Freud's limited focus on her. The first such example appears in Freud's primary account of Dora's mother. Dora's mother, Freud tells us, "had no understanding of her children's more active interests, and was occupied all day long in cleaning the house with its furniture and utensils and in keeping them clean—to such an extent as to make it almost impossible to use or enjoy them" (p. 20). Freud dismisses this cleaning as an obsession, but we might instead consider what a focus on cleaning to the "extent as to make [things] almost impossible to use or enjoy" tells us about desire. Here we have a sense of a type of jouissance that is beyond the phallic, and which is unknown. It is ex-timate in the sense that a woman cleaning a house might typically be seen as demonstrating a form of phallic jouissance, but the way the cleaning is approached suggests something more. What it suggests precisely appears unknown to Dora or indeed to her father—hence whilst she is located on the feminine side of the formula of sexuation, Dora's mother is not in the position of the not-all (for if she were, we would be much clearer about which particular part of her jouissance exceeds the phallic function).

The other example provided by Freud that affirms my suggestion that Dora's mother was in the position of the no exception appears in the following anecdote reported in the case:

Mother wanted to be given a particular thing—pearl drops to wear in her ears. But Father does not like that kind of thing, and he brought her a bracelet instead of the drops. She was furious, and told him that as he had spent so much money on a present she did not like he had better just give it to some one else. (p. 69)

It might be tempting to read this as a clear statement about Dora's mother's desire: that we know what she wants. But that, I would suggest, is a very simple and surface level reading, and even if it were treated as a clear indication of her desire, it wouldn't *per se* locate her as having access to a specific form of jouissance beyond the phallic. The point here is not that she wanted the pearl drops but got a bracelet instead. Rather, the point is that she wanted something beyond what was on offer to her: a piece of jouissance beyond that regulated by the phallus. Importantly, this anecdote about the pearl drops also gives us a vantage point from which to approach an understanding of the position of Dora's father.

At first glance we can read Dora's father on the masculine side of the formula of sexuation, specifically as the exception, who can insist (in the dream) upon his wife leaving her jewel box and who can ignore her wish for pearl drops and buy her a bracelet instead. Such a reading is contradicted, however, by Freud's emphasis in the case upon Dora's understanding that her father was impotent. This, then, is not a man who is an exception. Instead, this is a man in the position of the for-all, one who can enjoy certain women one at a time (the women before Dora's mother—from one of whom he contracted syphilis—Dora's mother, Frau K.).

Having identified Dora's mother in the position of the no exception, and her father in the position of the for-all, we can now turn to consider Dora's own position. From my explication of Dora's deciphering of her father's position, we can suggest that choosing a masculine positioning was not viable for Dora—it would not have given her access to that piece of her mother's desire that was beyond phallic jouissance and hence would not allow her to suture over the fact of the sexual non-relationship. Instead, I would suggest, Dora chose the position of the not-all. This is someone of whom part of their jouissance is beyond the phallic function. For Dora we can see this in her many forms of resistance. Her no to Herr K in the form of the slap at the lake, her reading of books, her attendance at lectures for women. This is a young woman who refused to entirely accept as her lot phallic jouissance: she refused her expected role as an exchange object in the dynamic between her parents and the Ks. Being in the position of the not-all also meant that Dora was potentially positioned to be that little piece of other jouissance for which her mother was reaching.

Of course this suggestion of mine contradicts Freud's depiction of Dora as hostile towards her mother. If, as Freud suggests, Dora showed little interest in her mother, why would we be convinced that she had chosen a position that afforded her a fantasy of access to her mother and the object a she represented? The answer to this, I believe, lies in the position of Frau K, though not in the form of homosexual desire as Freud's pink herring footnote would have us believe.

Instead, Frau K is the surrogate person Dora deciphers as being in the place of the no exception, and who thus stands in for her mother. Frau K. is the person who has a desire for something (otherwise why would she forgo intimacy with her husband, and instead pursue intimacy with a man who was impotent), but that desire is never clearly on the table. Frau K. is a person who knows something of desire beyond that regulated by the phallic function (hence her sharing of knowledge about sexual relations between men and women with Dora), but who nonetheless remains something of a mystery. Frau K. thus serves as a bridge between Dora's father (who can never give his wife what she wants) and her mother (who wants something that is unidentifiable). Whilst Dora's father similarly cannot give Frau K. what she wants (given that what she wants as the no exception is unidentifiable), she nonetheless provides to Dora a figure of the no exception in lieu of her mother through whom she can enjoy some form of relationship.

This then brings us to Herr K. In his book focusing on the case, Mahoney (1996) argues that Freud perpetuated Herr K.'s abuse of Dora by attempting to convince her that she was in love with Herr K. Whilst I am sympathetic to Mahoney's argument, and whilst I certainly do not wish to minimise the abuse of women in general (nor the specific ways in which Herr K.'s actions were inappropriate with regard to Dora), I do think there is more to be made of Dora's actions than is possible if we just reduce her to a victim of abuse. As I mentioned in the opening paragraph of this chapter, I believe that a specific focus on sexuation actually allows for a political reading of the case that affords agency to Dora.

As I have already established above, Dora chose the position of the not-all, and in so doing she established a claim to a form of jouissance beyond the phallic. This, of course, is not something we should reduce to a "political act": we are, after all, talking about unconscious fantasy here. Nonetheless, we can productively acknowledge that from this position Dora engaged in pursuits that brought with them a political aspect, such as her attending lectures for women. Reading Dora as the not-all also allows us to understand why Herr K., as the for-all, was not appealing to her. Not only was she not willing to be an exchange object, but she did not perceive him as someone capable of actually grasping anything beyond phallic jouissance. This provides us with some insight as to the slap at the lake: if Dora deciphered Herr K. as the for-all, then his overtures would likely have been inherently unappealing, incapable as he was of aiding her unconscious aim of accessing a piece of other jouissance.

The slap, following Gherovici (2010), potentially also tells us something more than just the position in which Herr K. was located. Not only was his position as the for-all unappealing, but the statement that preceded the slap—"I get nothing from my wife"—both reduced Frau K. as the no exception to a redundant object, and at the same time brought the role of Frau K. as exhibiting something of the object a all too clearly into view. In other words, not only did Herr K's statement threaten to bring asunder the role of Frau K. in Dora's fantasies of being a piece of other jouissance for her mother, but it also brought her too close to that fantasy. As we know from Lacan (2014), anxiety shows up in moments when the object a is activated: anxiety is about too much of the object a and the possibility of it being realised (which would then remove it from the realm of fantasy). The slap was thus a passage to the act in the sense that it stopped in its tracks the words that were possibly to come from Herr K.

What, then, can we say about the object a as it circulated in Dora's fantasy? As a first response to this question, we can return to the first dream documented above. Freud notes that "The [first] dream was a reaction to a fresh experience of an exciting nature; and this experience must inevitably have revived the memory of the only previous experience which was at all analogous to it" (p. 92). Freud tells us that whilst Dora had had this dream previously, she had it again in the days that followed the slap at the lake. I would suggest, then, that the "fresh" experience was an anxiety-producing encounter with the object a, a repetition of a previous encounter with it. A key to identifying the object *a* and the fantasy in which it is located must thus appear in the first dream. My suggestion is that the word "both" (as it appears in Mahoney's, 1996, translation) provides this key.

As writers such as Darian Leader (2000) have noted, in Freud's account of children's beating fantasies a child may not simply appear as one of the figures within a dream or fantasy. They may also appear as the very syntax of the fantasy or in its grammar. In Dora's recollection of the dream as recounted by Freud her father had said: "I don't want myself and both my children to be burnt up by fire because of your jewel box." My suggestion here is that whilst for Dora her father didn't want *both* of his children to be burnt up by fire, perhaps part of her fantasy was that *one* of his children would be burnt. Freud gives a positive interpretation of being burnt (linking it to sexual activity), but there is another positive interpretation to be made. Perhaps, instead of it being "your money or your life", the syntax of this part of the dream taking into account the "both" might be "your money (the jewel box) and *a* life".

At the end of the dream Dora is reported as stating that: "We hurried downstairs, and as soon as I was outside I woke up." So Dora escaped the fire, but what of her brother? Perhaps in the dream Dora's mother had to give up both her money and the life of her son, leaving her with what? Just Dora. This is a fantasy, then, in which Dora is positioned to be the remainder, which is precisely what the object *a* is: a remainder. In other words: Dora's deciphering of her mother's desire led her to the conclusion that what her mother wanted was something other than what she had (i.e., she didn't want her children, she wanted something more than them, as represented by her cleaning which made it so that objects such as furniture weren't useful for the purposes they were originally intended). What Dora needed to be, then, was a remainder. She needed to be something more than what is produced via a fantasy of oneness between a caregiver and child. She needed to be what falls to the wayside.

The second dream helps us to unpack this desire to be what remains. Below I include first Strachey's translation and then Mahoney's (1996):

> I was walking about in a town which I did not know. I saw streets and squares which were strange to me. Then I came into a house where I lived, went to my room, and found a letter from Mother

lying there. She wrote saying that as I had left home without my parents' knowledge she had not wished to write to me to say that Father was ill "Now he is dead, and if you like you can come" I then went to the station and asked about a hundred times: "Where is the station?" I always got the answer: "Five minutes". I then saw a thick wood before me which I went into, and there I asked a man whom I met. He said to me: "Two and a half hours more." He offered to accompany me. But I refused and went alone. I saw the station in front of me and could not reach it. At the same time I had the usual feeling of anxiety that one has in dreams when one cannot move forward. Then I was at home. I must have been travelling in the meantime, but I know nothing about that. I walked into the porter's lodge, and enquired for our flat. The maidservant opened the door to me and replied that Mother and the others were already at the cemetery. (p. 94)

I go walking in a city that I do not know, and I see streets and squares that are strange to me. Then I come into a house where I live, go to my room, and find Mama's letter lying there. She writes: Since I am away from home without my parents' knowledge, she didn't wish to write to me that Papa took ill. Now he has died, and if you want, you can come. So I go to the station and ask perhaps 100 times: Where is the station? I always receive the answer: Five minutes. Then I see a thick wood in front of me and I go into it and ask a man whom I meet there. He says to me: 2 ½ hours more. He offers to accompany me. I refuse and go alone. I see the station in front of me and cannot reach it. At the same time I have the usual feeling of anxiety that one gets when one cannot go farther in a dream. Then I am home; in the meantime I must have travelled but I know nothing about that. I step into the porter's lodge and ask him about our apartment. The maidservant opens for me and replies: Your mom and the others are already at the cemetery. (p. 87)

The first point of note in this dream is the fact that the letter from her mother tells Dora that her father is dead. Dora's brother is not mentioned at all. So Dora is finally the remainder in her family, the one piece left behind for her mother. We then have the man who offers help but whose help is redundant to Dora in the dream. This, I would suggest, is Herr K. As I outlined above, he is useless to Dora as a means of accessing the desire of Frau K. and hence the desire of her mother. Dora then reports a feeling of anxiety, so we must ask if the object *a* is in sight. Just when it appears in the dream that Dora has become the remainder, she cannot reach it—it is right in front of her but still eludes her (and this is the nature of the no exception itself, the piece of other jouissance contained in this position is elusive).

Yet we might also ask if the anxiety in the dream is about Dora's proximity to having what she wants; whether her anxiety is both about the fact that her opportunity to become her mother's remainder is so close and yet so far, but also precisely *because* it is so close. The dream resolves this dilemma of desiring but not wanting to have what she desires by the quick switch to "then I am home", but a home where her mother is not. Her mother (and hence her mother's desire) is still some distance away. Indeed, we could suggest that there is something to be made of the fact that her mother is at the cemetery. Certainly, her mother being at the cemetery fits with the fact that in the dream she wrote to tell Dora that her father was dead. But beyond that, her mother not being at home and instead being at the cemetery is perhaps a reminder to Dora that coming too close to her desire risks ending up at the cemetery and the death of her desire.

Conclusions

In his analysis of the "Fragment of an analysis of a case of hysteria" Freud makes much of a range of associations between jewellery, female genitalia, and Dora's relationship with her father and Herr K. In a footnote to the postscript, however, he introduces a third person into this allegedly heated set of conscious and unconscious sexual exchanges: Frau K. I have argued, contrarily, that the very person who disappears from the Freud's report of the case—Dora's mother—is the person to whom we should be looking to understanding Dora's position in terms of sexuation, her object *a*, and the fantasy within which it sits. This is not to say that the other characters in the story are irrelevant. Clearly as I have elaborated above, each played a role in Dora's working through of her own position and her access to her object *a*. Bringing in a focus on Dora's mother, however, allows us to further unpack the two dreams and the slap at the lake.

Also as I have noted briefly in this chapter, focusing on sexuation allows us to understand something of the politics of Dora's life as a young woman, located as she was in the position of the not-all. Whilst this does not give a prescription for all people similarly located in this position, and nor does it necessarily give us further purchase upon Dora's symptoms, it does allow us to think about the political within a Lacanian framework, a point I return to in the final chapter of this book.

Whilst much has been made, including by Lacan (2007), of Freud's misreading of the transference in his work with Dora, the analysis I have presented in this chapter provides us with further analytic leverage for thinking about what might have happened had Freud taken a different tack in attempting to decipher Dora's desire. Beyond this type of revisionist historical work, however, the outcomes of any analysis are likely to be considerably different if a focus on sexuation is included, as it provides us with a particular set of coordinates for thinking about the production of desire. This is a topic that I will explore in depth in the final chapter of this book.

CHAPTER FIVE

Analysis of a phobia in a five-year-old boy

The case

In many ways, Freud's (1909b) case reporting an "Analysis of a phobia in a five-year-old boy" is the most difficult to write about in the context of the theoretical framework that I offer in this book. Whilst in the case of "The psychogenesis of a case of homosexuality in a woman" there was relatively little analytic material (and specifically no dreams) to work with, the material that is available is rich in meaning. Certainly in Freud's "Analysis of a phobia in a five-year-old boy" the material is rich, but at the same time it is limited first by the fact that the analysis was not conducted by Freud (instead, it was conducted by the boy's father, and then reported by Freud), and it is also limited by the fact that the child was so young, and hence the analytic material that he provided is relatively limited. Nonetheless, as we shall see below, much has been made of the case in previous accounts, and I believe that there is something novel to be made of the case by focusing on sexuation.

Before discussing the case itself, as I noted above the analysis (if we can call it that) was undertaken by the boy's father. Whilst Freud met with the boy and his father and gave directions to the latter in terms of particular avenues to pursue, almost all of the material presented in the case is derived either from conversations the father had with his son, or accounts provided by the son about his daily activities and his day-dreams. As a result of relying on second hand information, to a certain extent the presentation of the case by Freud is somewhat less dynamic than the presentation of his other cases. Much of the case material is presented as interchanges between the father and son as reported to Freud by the former. This can in places be quite mundane and in many ways over determined, a point that Freud himself notes in his sugges-tion that at times the father makes too much of a particular comment from his son.

As a reader, each time I have read the case there have certainly been moments when I am left wondering whether the father was too focused on attempting to analyse his son, and as a result made analytic specula-tions that were not warranted by what his son was saying. This is not to say that children are not speakingbeings and that they cannot provide us with interesting analytic material. Rather, my point is that when we are dealing with a person who has not *per se* asked for an analysis, it is difficult to draw the line between what often appear to be standard conversations between a parent and a child, and what are often taken to be conversations between an analyst and an analysand.

Furthermore, and as I will discuss below, Ross (2007) alleges that in his focus on undertaking an analysis, the father failed to see what was happening in his own home. Ross alleges that the mother was abusing both her son and her daughter, and that the son was telling his father about this. The father, Ross suggests, failed to hear what the son was saying because he was so focused on their conversations as sources of analytic material, and thus treated much of what his son said as fan-tasy, rather than potentially as concrete claims about actual abuse. Ross draws upon interviews undertaken with the son and father when they were adults, interviews that have in the past decade become publically available. As I will discuss below, I think the account that Ross provides is perhaps a little over determined and too strong in its claims, but it nonetheless offers yet another vantage point on why the case itself is difficult to engage with analytically.

In terms of the case, the five-year-old boy is known as Little Hans, though in real life he was Herbert Graf. Given the case is well known as the case of Little Hans, for the purposes of this chapter I will retain the pseudonym used by Freud. The events of the case, whilst span-ning many pages, are relatively brief. As the eldest child of two, for the first three years of his life Hans appeared to have enjoyed a relatively happy life, and was reported to be an amiable young person. His family enjoyed holidays in the country where Hans enjoyed friendships with local children. His happiness in life, however, was tempered upon the birth of a sister when Han was three. We are told that Hans showed much curiosity about where his sister came from (having been given the tale of the "stork" to account for the birth of a child), and also that he was quite vocal about wishing that she hadn't been born. Both of Hans' parents, along with Freud, also emphasised the obsession that Hans apparently showed about his own penis and that of others (though importantly, as we shall see below, the word that is reported in the case in German in wiwimacher, though Strachey translates this as widdler, which to a large degree changes the word from a descriptor of a body part that produces urine—so a urethra—to a penis), and also Hans' alleged obsession with masturbation.

With all of these varying events and alleged obsessions in play, the scene is then set in the case for the development of a phobia. This, we are told, is a phobia of horses, following an event where Hans was out walking with his mother and saw a horse fall over whilst pulling a bus. This phobia becomes generalised to all horses and also to some other large animals (such as elephants and giraffes), to the point where Hans is unable to leave the house for fear of seeing a horse. Much of the case is focused on attempting to decipher this phobia around horses, and the emphasis is placed by both the father and Freud upon an association between horses and the father, and the prohibition the latter placed on Hans coming into bed with his mother in the mornings. By the end of the case report, we are told that the phobia had abated, and that Hans was freed of his phobia of horses and in the process had worked through his desire to understand the differences between male and female bodies, and how children are born. As we shall see in the following section, much that has been previously written about the case has challenged the coordinates of the case outlined above, and in varying ways what has been written previously touches on issues that I will examine more closely in my analysis of the case.

Previous accounts

Perhaps of all of the bodies of work that sit around each of Freud's cases, the body of work that has focused on Freud's "Analysis of a phobia in a five-year-old boy" is the one that most closely aligns with my own reading of the case. This is not to say that I necessarily agree with all that has been written about the case (as we shall see shortly), and certainly none of what has been previously written focuses explicitly on the formula of sexuation (though an excellent article written by Pluth (2007) does focus on Lacan's account of the sexual non-relation in regards to the case). Nonetheless, as we shall now see, other writers have picked up elements of the case that I too believe warrant further attention.

One of the previous accounts that is arguably most unlike my own is provided by Corbett (2009). Through his focus on the construction of masculinity in the case, Corbett "place[s] considerable value on the role of fantasy as it builds the boy" (p. 736), and specifically he suggests that the phobia about the falling horse was a fantasy that helped Hans explain the "*lack* of desire and authority" (p. 756, original emphasis) in the household. Certainly there is something to be made of the lack of physical desire between the mother and father, a point that Ross (2007) emphasises in his reading of both the case and the interviews undertaken with Hans and his father many years later. Corbett, however, appears to overstate the case by suggesting that there was a lack of desire, in that he appears to conflate conscious desire (specifically with reference to desiring intimacy with a partner) with unconscious desire.

Despite this apparent misreading in regards to desire in the case, I would concur with Corbett (2009) that there was something of a lack of authority, specifically with regard to the "no" of the father. Despite Freud's endorsement of the father (understandable given the father was an acolyte), and despite what appears to be the father's belief that he was in a position of authority—that he embodied the position of the subject supposed to know, in Lacan's terms—there are certainly instances in the case where Hans appears to decipher his father as not necessarily in a position of authority. This is a point I will return to in my analysis of the case.

Ross (2007) similarly takes up the topic of the authority of the father, and in no uncertain terms suggests that the father failed as an authority figure as he failed to understand that his son was verbalising to him the abuse he was being subjected to by his mother. As I noted above, Ross makes these claims through his readings of both the case and the interviews undertaken with Hans and his father when the former was an adult. Ross is adamant that the mother abused both of her children, and perhaps especially her daughter. He suggests that this abuse was sexual (the mother exposing herself to her son), physical (the mother smacking both of her children), and emotional (the mother demanding love from her son and showing no regard for her daughter). Ross specifically suggests that the mother was to blame for any lack of authority held by the father, as can be seen in the following quote:

> Perhaps her son also served as a phallic narcissistic extension of her otherwise damaged self [...]. While her many declarations that she does have a "widdler" might very well be seen as a "proto-feminist" assertion that, yes, she possesses a female genital or for that matter a urethra, they may also betray an unconscious fantasy that she has a male organ tucked up inside her and/or projected onto her boy (You, Hans, are my widdler!). Moreover, she seems to have taunted her husband with this new plaything, in the process devaluing the boy's father in his eyes. (p. 788)

This quote is indicative of the type of hyperbole evident throughout all of Ross' article, hyperbole in many places that rests to a certain degree upon what I believe to be an over-reading of the case materials. Certainly the same accusation can be levelled at Freud, who in his discussion makes claims that, at least in my reading, far exceed the analytic material. Ross' agenda, however, is different to Freud's, in that his aim is to show that child abuse occurred in the Graf household, and that no one listened when Hans attempted to disclose this. My point here is not to dispute this possibility, but rather to question the methods by which Ross makes his claims. Whilst child abuse understandably evokes strong feelings, its investigation requires care. Instead, I would suggest that Ross' writing is itself another form of violence, not only in its insistence upon abuse in very particular ways, but also in its failure to locate the abuse in a particular familial and historical context (i.e., the mother is accused of abuse, whilst the father is largely absolved of abuse, albeit he is depicted as an accomplice due to his failure to hear what Hans was saying).

Moving on from Ross (2007), three writers (including Corbett, 2009, already mentioned above) elaborate an account of the case that provides some of the coordinates that I will investigate in my analysis below. Starting with Corbett, he suggests that Freud's emphasis on Hans' desire for his mother marginalises a specific aspect of Hans' identification with his father. Both Freud and Hans' father focus primarily on the anger that Hans had for his father, alleging that Hans wished to supplant his father's role in the household so that he could have his mother. Corbett, by contrast, suggests that what Hans wanted was to be a father with children. In this sense, whilst in Corbett's account Hans very much did want to supplant his father, it was not *per se* so that he could have his mother. Rather, it was so that he could have children.

As per my critique of Corbett's (2009) account earlier, however, I would again suggest that his account of Hans' desire to have children is limited. I would agree that it would appear that Hans wanted to have children, but I would not agree necessarily that he desired to be a father who had children in the way that his own father did. One of the many questions that remains from the case is how Hans understood the role of fathers in terms of having children. Whilst Freud suggests that Hans had something of an understanding of how children are conventionally conceived (through heterosex) and how they are birthed vaginally, I would not be so quick to presume that Hans as a child believed that these were the only ways to have a child.

Rudnytsky (2000) suggests as much in his account of the case, in which he proposes that Hans "desire[d] not simply to marry but to *be* Mommy. The child's identifications are multiple, maternal as well as paternal" (p. 45). As we shall see below, I believe that this account is still somewhat simplistic (in that it perpetuates the interpretation that Hans desired to marry his mother, and simply adds to this the idea he wanted to be her). It is simplistic, I would suggest, because whilst it accepts that Hans wanted to have a child, it treats as an *a priori* the fact that a child who does not have a uterus can never birth a child. In other words, what it accepts is a biological impossibility, and thus Rudnytsky's account is forced to suggest that Hans wanted to be his mother. There is another account possible if we make a shift away from identification understood in terms of grounded in the "reality" of bodies, and to instead focus on an understanding of sexuation where the ways in which a child interprets the desire of a first Other and how they attempt to navigate the sexual non-relationship is a question of fantasy, not "reality".

Despite these concerns about Rudnytsky's (2000) account, there are still aspects of it that warrant further attention. Both Rudnytsky and Pluth (2007) suggest that what Hans saw in his mother was a fundamental ambivalence about childbirth. Specifically, Rudnytsky focuses on a portion of the case where Hans discusses information that he had gained from his mother about how children come to be, information that can easily be read as suggesting first that his mother only had children because God intended it to be, and subsequently would only have a third child if it was both God's and her own intent. This is a woman, then, whose relationship to being a mother is opaque—it is never clear in the case (or I would suggest in Hans' mind at the time) whether children were actually what his mother desired.

Pluth (2007) takes this point about the mother's ambivalence further, when he states:

> The primary importance of this symbolic event [of Hans' mother refusing to touch his penis whilst drying him after a bath] lies in the way in which it reveals to Hans that his position with respect to his mother's desire is not what he might have thought. Lacan's discussion of the implications of this episode focuses on how it enables Hans to see that her desire is partly directed toward something other than him, something other than what he has always presumed desire to be about—what we call the imaginary phallus. He starts suspecting, then, that he does not complete his mother at all. In that imaginary game, it was Hans's belief that it was he himself, his very being, that satisfied her. Her refusal of his penis leads Hans to conclude that something about it, and him, is inadequate and miserable. (p. 74)

In his paper more broadly Pluth elaborates Lacan's account of the sexual non-relation and suggests that part of what was at stake for Hans was the fact that his mother's actions led him to see that there was no oneness with her: he did not complete her. This point is one that I now take up in my analysis of the case, focusing on the positions of Hans and his parents (as it would appear he deciphered the latter to be), the fantasy in which those positions circulated, and the ways in which the fantasy allowed Hans access to his object *a*.

A focus on sexuation

As we can see from my summary in the previous section, whilst Freud made much in the case of talk between Hans and his parents about "widdlers", writing that has since focused on the case has tended to focus less on the equation of "widdler talk" with Hans' penis and thus less on castration anxiety in a Freudian sense. Interestingly, in a footnote added to the case fourteen years after it was published, Freud noted that others who had since written about the castration complex focused more on castration as the loss of a sense of oneness with the mother, rather than as fear of physical castration *per se*. Yet despite this, in the footnote Freud continues to insist that the "Analysis of a phobia in a five-year-old boy" was centrally about castration anxiety in terms of the penis itself (p. 8, fn. 2).

I would suggest that this insistent focus upon castration in terms of the penis was, at least in the context of this case, a pink herring. In his discussion about the case, Freud notes that:

> In those who later become homosexuals we meet with the same predominance in infancy of the genital zone (and especially of the penis) as in normal persons. Indeed it is the high esteem felt by the homosexual for the male organ which decides his fate. In his child-hood he chooses women as his sexual object, so long as he assumes that they too possess what in his eyes is an indispensable part of the body; when he becomes convinced that women have deceived him in this particular, they cease to be acceptable to him as a sexual object. He cannot forgo a penis in any one who is to attract him to sexual intercourse; and if circumstances are favourable he will fix his libido upon the "woman with a penis", a youth of feminine appearance. (p. 109)

Whilst Freud stops short of directly applying this logic to Hans, certainly throughout the case he makes references to Hans' homosexuality (though notably not in reference to his focus on "widdlers", but rather more in terms of his affection for other boys). This equation of a pre-dominance of the genital zone with homosexuality is, I would suggest, a pink herring. Importantly, my suggestion is not that for some gay men the genital zone does not predominate. But this is not exclusive to gay men. What Freud conflates is a particular object *a* (the penis, or something about it), identification, and sexuation. To move past this pink herring, then, we need to unpack in detail sexuation as it appears in the case.

Perhaps the simplest place to start is the position of the father as deciphered by Hans. As I noted earlier in this chapter, whilst the case as presented is quite long, the analytic material is relatively brief, and much of it is provoked by the father through long series of questions. What I largely focus on here are the daydreams that Hans reported to his father, and other observations that he appeared to have made relatively independent of this questioning. There are two daydreams in particular that I would suggest give us some insight as to how Hans deciphered the position of his father. These are the two daydreams as the father reported them to Freud:

> On Monday, March 30th, in the morning, Hans came to me and said: "I say! I thought two things this morning!" "What was the first?" "I was with you at Schonbrunn where the sheep are; and then we crawled through under the ropes, and then we told the policeman at the end of the garden, and he grabbed hold of us". (p. 40)
>
> After we returned from our visit to you [...] Hans confessed to yet another little bit of craving to do something forbidden: "I say, I thought something this morning again". "What?" "I went with you in the train, and we smashed a window and the policeman took us off with him". (p. 41)

Both Freud and the father interpret these little thoughts as suggesting that Hans identified with his father, and specifically that he identified with certain violent and illicit acts that his father engaged in. Freud (I believe over-) extrapolates from this to suggest that the daydreams were metaphors for penetration—that these were Hans' attempts at grappling with the operations of heterosex. I don't actually accept this interpretation, for many reasons. First, Freud had no evidence to suggest that Hans had any knowledge of heterosex. Second, Freud treats it as axiomatic that a boy would want to put his penis in something—this to me is both unnecessarily sexualising and with the presumption that the something is a vagina, heterosexist. Finally, and my key point here, is that I think the interpretation refuses to acknowledge that in both daydreams the attempt at violence/penetration is thwarted.

In making this last point, my suggestion is that Hans deciphered his father as being in the position of the for-all. This was not a person who was the exception—he did not have unmitigated access to anything (including any woman). As we can see in the daydreams, this is a person who, when attempting to go somewhere forbidden or do something illegal, is caught. This is thus a person fully caught within the phallic function. Beyond these particular daydreams, whilst so much of the analytic material is about the father, this is largely because *it was the father asking the questions:* so many of the questions he asked were about himself. Even in another dream which the father interprets as being about himself as situated in a position of authority, in fact this was not how Hans interpreted it. In this dream, Hans tells his father:

> In the night there was a big giraffe in the room and a crumpled one; and the big one called out because I took the crumpled one away from it. Then it stopped calling out; and then I sat down on top of the crumpled one. (p. 37)

Both Freud and the father interpret the big giraffe as the father and the crumpled one as the mother, thus claiming that the father has authority over the mother. This is despite the fact that the father tells Freud that the next day, as he left the house, he made a joke of the dream by saying "goodbye giraffe" to his wife as he left the house. Hans asked him why he did this, and the father said that the mother was the big giraffe, to which Hans replied that his sister was the crumpled giraffe. The father, then, by Hans' understanding, was neither of the giraffes. Again, then, this is not a person in a position of absolute authority, nor would it appear that this is a person who has access to any form of jouissance other than the phallic. Instead, this is a person wholly within the phallic function—the for-all.

Having established this claim about Hans' deciphering of the position of his father, we can now turn to consider his deciphering of the position of the mother. As I noted above in terms of the work of both Rudnytsky (2000) and Pluth (2007), it would appear that Hans perceived his mother as ambivalent about having children, and ambivalent about her desire for Hans himself. I will state clearly now that the position I believe Hans deciphered his mother as being in was that of the no-exception. Let us now explore in detail how I came to this conclusion.

Unpacking how Hans potentially deciphered the position of his mother requires navigating a range of comments about her and a number of related comments that weave throughout the case. Before doing so, however, it might be useful for the reader to provide an overview of these events in the order in which they must be understood. Importantly, whilst I will provide an account of these events in chronological order (rather than necessarily in the order they are presented in the case), it is vital to understand as with any analysis that chronological order is not the key. Rather, the key is how events may be retrospectively interpreted and given a specific meaning that potentially differs from the meaning that may have existed at the first time of the event.

The first key event appears to have happened when Hans was three, before his sister was born. The family had travelled to Gmunden to holiday, and whilst there Hans had played with neighbourhood children. During this time, the following event occurred, as related to Freud by the father:

I: "Used you often to play at horses [whilst at Gmunden]?"
HANS: "Very often. Fritzl was the horse once, too, and Franzl the coachman; and Fritzl ran ever so fast and all at once he hit his foot on a stone and bled.

Fritzl and Franzl are pet names for two boys who Hans often played with at Gmunden. In this particular event, they were playing horses (a game involving one person being the horse, and another person being the driver steering the horse). In this particular instance of the game that Hans witnessed, Fritzl was the horse, and stubbed his toe and it bled. The bleeding here is the key part of the event, though of course in its association with a horse (here Fritzl playing at being one).

The next event of significance is the birth of a sister—Hanna. There are many discussions in the case about this event, and much extrapolation from these discussions by Freud and the father about the meaning of pregnancy, birth and conception for Hans. What I wish to focus on here is the brief summary of the day of the birth itself, specifically:

[After his sister was born at home in his parents' bedroom, Hans] was then called into the bedroom. He did not look at his mother, however, but at the basins and other vessels, filled with blood and water, that were still standing about the room. Pointing to the blood-stained bed-pan, he observed in a surprised voice: "But blood doesn't come out of *my* widdler." (p. 10, original emphasis)

Here we have another encounter with blood, this time in the context of childbirth, and Hans' assumption that blood in the bed-pan must mean that someone had urinated blood into the bed-pan. Clearly here Hans does not have the information necessary to understand why there is blood during childbirth, and where the blood comes from. Importantly, however, his emphasis upon blood coming from a "widdler" connects to his mother in a very specific way, despite the incorrect nature of his knowledge about childbirth. Previously Hans had told his mother that he was trying to see if she had a "widdler too", to which she replied "of course", which prompted Hans to say "I thought you were so big you'd have a widdler like a horse" (p. 10). So in this little exchange we have the mother, the horse, and the "widdler" all together, and combined with the story about childbirth and blood in the bed-pan, the five (mother, horse, "widdler", childbirth, blood) coalesce into one grouping of meanings. In his discussion of the case, Freud makes this same grouping in his statement that:

> We can now recognise that all furniture-vans and drays and buses were only stork-box carts, and were only of interest to Hans as being symbolic representations of pregnancy; and that when a heavy or heavily loaded horse fell down he can have seen in it only one thing—a childbirth, a delivery. Thus the falling horse was not only his dying father but also his mother in childbirth. (p. 128)

Putting all of this together, then, we can make a statement about Hans' deciphering of the position of his mother. Here is a person who shows ambivalence about having children and being a mother, and yet despite this ambivalence, is willing to be the horse who falls, the one who bleeds. For Hans, when Fritzl stubbed his toe and it bled, this was not a pleasant occurrence to witness. Similarly, his supposition that the blood in the bed-pan was from his mother's "widdler" does not appear to have been a positive occurrence for him either. Yet his mother, it would appear, is willing to be the horse who bleeds. This, then, is a person who desires something beyond that which Hans can know, a little bit of something we might conjecture that is beyond phallic jouissance— a pleasure in something that Hans can only perceive as unpleasant. This is a person in the position of the no-exception, one who has access to an other jouissance that is indeterminate.

Our question now, then, is what did this mean for Hans? How did he make a choice in terms of sexuation that allowed him to navigate the sexual non-relationship; to perpetuate the fantasy of oneness with his mother? And further what was the fantasy in which this sexuated position circulated, and where in it did his object *a* potentially lie? Taking into account Pluth's (2007) suggestion that in varying ways Hans received the message from his mother that *he* was not the object cause of her desire, we need to acknowledge how despite this Hans potentially attempted to decipher what he could give his mother. My answer to this question is that his fantasy involved having a child for his mother— that if, despite her ambivalence, she continued to have children, Hans saw this as something she might want. This positions Hans, then, in the place of the not-all: as the person who can have a little bit of other jouissance that is known (i.e., both to give his mother what he thinks she wants, and to be able to do so as a child without a uterus).

We first learn of Hans' perception that he has children in a story related by his father:

> In the winter (at the age of three and three-quarters) I took Hans to the skating rink and introduced him to my friend N.'s two little daughters, who were about ten years old. Hans sat down beside them, while they, in the consciousness of their mature age, looked down on the little urchin with a good deal of contempt; he gazed at them with admiration, though this proceeding made no great impression on them. In spite of this Hans always spoke of them afterwards as "my little girls". "Where are my little girls? When are my little girls coming?" And for some weeks he kept tormenting me with the question: "When am I going to the rink again to see my little girls?" (p. 15)

We could, of course, dismiss this reference to the children as "his girls" as a term of endearment made by a small child. The father, however, also thought there was something more to this than terms of endearment. At a later date he questioned Hans extensively about his belief that he had or would have children. The interchange that followed the initial question of why he was always thinking of "his" children went as follows:

HANS: Why? Because I should so like to have children; but I don't ever want it; I shouldn't like to have them.

I: Have you always imagined that Berta and Olga and the rest were your children?

HANS: Yes. Franzl, and Fritzl, and Paul too (his playmates at Lainz), and Lodi.' […].

      I: So you thought you were their Mummy?
HANS: And really I was their Mummy.
      I: But who did you think you'd got the children from?
HANS: Why, from me.
      I: You had Grete in bed with you yesterday, but you know quite
          well that boys can't have children.
HANS: Well, yes. But I believe they can, all the same.

This truncated version of a longer set of exchanges condenses the comments that Hans made about having children. Here we can see his own ambivalence: he believes he can have children from himself, despite knowing that boys can't have children, yet at the same time he doesn't want to have them. I would suggest that this is a vocalisation of his fantasy at play, and the importance of the fantasy as opposed to any reality. The fantasy is that he could have a child from himself, and thus be the Mummy. Importantly, I do not share Rudnytsky's (2000) interpretation that Hans wanted to be *his* mother. Rather, my interpretation is that he wanted to be a mother *for* his mother. In other words, he would have children for her—that he would give her the mysterious thing that she appeared to both want but not necessarily want.

An important point of clarification comes in the first sentence in the quote above, when Hans says "I don't want ever it". This "it", I believe, is important. Whilst he then goes on to talk about actual children, I would hesitate in taking the "it" as referring to actual children. Instead, I would suggest that the "it" is pregnancy and childbirth. In other words, Hans wants to have children for himself and his mother, but he doesn't want to be the fallen horse who bleeds. His fantasy, then, is of being a progenitor in a form of an immaculate conception: he doesn't need anyone else to have children, and he doesn't have to be pregnant or give birth, he can just have children at will. This is a fantasy that accords him some kind of relationship to his mother in the face of the sexual non-relationship; a connection to her that allows him to feel a oneness with her in their united bond as people who have children.

This then brings us to the question of the object *a* that circulates within this fantasy. Like much analytic work, my suggestion is that the answer lies within the syntax of the fantasy itself, as a paired opposite of the fantasy. In other words, whilst the fantasy is one that involves a claim to oneness with the mother through a shared experience of mothering, underpinning this, I would suggest, is precisely the opposite: the desire to not share anything with the mother. This might seem contradictory (i.e., why have a fantasy that props up an object *a* which it contradicts). However, as I will now elaborate, it is not contradictory, but rather is complementary. To state it simply first, the object *a* was his mother's ambivalence. The fantasy attempts to locate that ambivalence in a context that is somewhat less ambivalent, precisely because the ambivalence that his mother displayed undermined his claim to connection with her.

Throughout the case much is made by both Freud and the father about Hans' reported desire to "coax" with his mother. This word is of course Strachey's translation, with other possible translations being "flatter", "caress", and "have intentions towards". We are told in the case that Hans was anxious about not being about to "coax" with his mother, and that often in response to his phobia of horses he sought to "coax" with his mother. In his seminar on anxiety, Lacan (2010) notes that anxiety is caused when the object *a* is too close. Specifically with reference to maternal presence, Lacan suggests that anxiety is produced when there is *no* gap between the mother and the child, rather than when there is too little gap.

From this logic presented by Lacan, we can suggest that perhaps whilst consciously Hans sought to "coax" with his mother, unconsciously perhaps his anxiety was about the lack of separation from his mother (who was, after all, the horse who bled—the cause of his phobia). The object *a*, then, is a certain sense of ambivalence evoked in relation to the mother. On the one hand, Hans sought ways to approximate his object *a*, but of course on the other hand he did not want to approximate it (at least in part because his mother's ambivalence involved him, but also because the object *a* is a source of anxiety—having access to one's jouissance is anxiety producing). The fantasy of having a child for his mother whilst also not having a child for his mother thus allowed this ambivalence to circulate for Hans—to keep his desire in play.

Conclusions

Despite the relative lack of analytic material, and the ways in which the case was over-determined by the role of the father as analyst, in this chapter we can see that even with these constraints, something can be identified in terms of the operations of sexuation. Admittedly, this requires leaving to one side much of what Freud and the father made of the case (specifically, their focus on castration and "widdlers"). This, however, is understandable, given the fact that a focus on sexuation is largely a Lacanian formulation, and one that requires us to view the case from a different vantage point.

It is notable that whilst previous accounts of the case have often taken it as a prime example of the interpolation of a boy into discourses of masculinity (indeed, Connell, 2000, suggests that the Little Hans case constitutes the seminal grounds for the study of boys and masculinity), my analysis has suggested that Hans was potentially located on the feminine side of the formula of sexuation. Of course, having been assigned male, identifying as a male, engaging in masculine behaviours, and being interpolated by norms of masculinity don't necessary have anything to do with sexuation—this is precisely Lacan's point. Nonetheless, it is notable that when we step outside of these types of categorisation, we can potentially see different aspects of a case that, I would argue, may ultimately be more useful than simply focusing on what is presumed to be obvious.

To a certain degree this is all moot, given the case occurred a long time ago and my analysis of it will not change anything about the case. Nonetheless, and as I will discuss in further detail in the final chapter of this book, what we can take from my analysis of the case is the fact that normative presumptions about children are likely to only take us so far. Instead, what is required are careful examinations of how children understand their positioning within the context of their families, and how they decipher the desire of their first Other in a relationship to the "no" of a second Other. Whilst we must be cautious in inferring any type of relationship between the two that would see them as complementary (i.e., which would suggest that two particular sexuated positions "naturally" go together), we can nonetheless consider how modes of jouissance coalesce together and how this speaks less to any claim to overcoming the sexual non-relationship, and more to how certain modes of jouissance seek their fulfilment in fantasies that are shaped by the relationships between children and their caregivers.

CHAPTER SIX

Notes upon a case of obsessional neurosis

The case

At last we come to Freud's (1909d) "Notes upon a case of obsessional neurosis", the case I discussed at the beginning of this book as one that shaped my early thinking about the concept of pink herrings. In returning to my copy of the case I found that I had indeed marked instances throughout where Freud uses words such as "anus", "buttocks", "rectum", and "arse" to discuss the key coordinates of the case as he saw them. As we know by this point of the book, my focus will not specifically be on these words. Indeed, my early interest in them was something of a pink herring itself. Nonetheless, into the future there is most definitely a study to be made of how both Freud and Lacan, when discussing the case, variously use these words in ways that potentially have something to tell us about their own positionings in addition to what each of the terms have to tell us about the neuroses of Ernst Lanzer, the analysand who is the focus of the case.

In terms of my analytic focus in this chapter, and as I have said with regard to other chapters in this book, the case itself is relatively thin in terms of analytic material that would allow us to focus even more closely on sexuation. Fortunately for us, however, the Standard Edition includes excerpts from Freud's original case notes. These are replete with dreams that Freud, with his primary focus on the other aspects of the case materials, did not discuss in the case report itself. It is these additional materials presented in the original case notes that I will primarily consider in my analysis below.

In terms of the broad details of the case, Ernst Lanzer presented to Freud with two interrelated symptoms: a fear that a particular torture was going to be applied to two people he loved (his father, who was at the time of the analysis deceased, and the woman he loved and desired to marry and whom he later did marry), and a series of compulsive injunctions or rituals that he felt compelled to perform. These rituals included prayers to ward off particular thoughts, obsessive exercise, the thought that he should cut his throat, and a wish that the aforementioned torture *should* be applied to his loved ones. We will explore the torture in more detail below, but we can note here that Ernst first heard about it whilst he was an officer in the army reserve, where a captain known for his cruel ways recounted the story of a particular form of "eastern torture" to a group of officers. Whilst the after effects of hearing about this torture were significant and became the central focus of Freud's analysis of Ernst, the torture itself (one involving rats—hence the "Rat man" moniker often appended to the case) actually evoked earlier fears that Ernst had of rats.

These earlier fears, we learn from the case, arose from a complex series of early life experiences. Ernst was both fortunate to have lived in a house where his parents were, for the large part, happily married. Nonetheless, as we shall see below, particular dynamics in terms of the arrangement of the marriage—which was then mirrored in attempts at arranging a marriage for Ernst—brought forth for Ernst a range of fears related to the extent to which bodies are truly bounded, and their permeability. This was specifically the case in regards to the relationships that Ernst experienced with women who worked for his family (i.e., household staff), in addition to his own mother, and his other female relatives. There is a sense in the case that Ernst both experienced a lack of boundaries with these female figures in his life, yet at the same time was bound by a very formulaic set of relationships between himself and the girls and women in his life as a young boy. Before moving on to present my analysis of the case, we can first consider how other writers have understood the key coordinates of the case.

Previous accounts

Much of what has been previously written about Freud's "Notes upon a case of obsessional neurosis" has seemingly taken for granted the pairing of latent homosexuality, anal eroticism, and feminine identification. To a certain extent, then, previous accounts of the case mirror previous accounts of "From the history of an infantile neurosis", substituting the wolf for the rat. As I argued in chapter four with regard to Freud's "From the history of an infantile neurosis", this emphasis upon homosexuality and anal eroticism constitute something of a pink herring, and I would suggest that this emphasis has prevented a closer analysis of other aspects of the case materials.

With regard to a focus on homosexuality, Kassabian and Kazanjian (2005, p. 133) suggest that Freud's focus on a positive resolution to the Oedipus complex in the case elides what they see as the installation of "a particularly volatile prohibition against homosexual object-choice" arising from an "ambivalent mixture of love and hatred directed" by Ernst towards his father. They specifically suggest that one particular shared family narrative, which involved Ernst being punished by his father at a young age for biting someone, evoked a "paternal assertion of mastery and power" that was then later repeated in the story of the torture told by the cruel captain. Specifically, Kassabian and Kazanjian suggest that the story of the torture—in which "'the criminal was tied up [...] a pot was turned upside down on his buttocks [...] some *rats* were put into it [...] and they [...] *bored their way in* [...].' Into his anus" (Freud, 1909d, p. 166)—enacted a second prohibition on homosexuality experienced by Ernst. Whilst I would agree with Kassabian and Kazanjian that Freud's emphasis upon a positive resolution to the Oedipus complex is somewhat limited, I do not share their view that the limit is a result of the lack of focus upon a prohibition on homosexuality, as we shall see in my analysis below.

Mahoney (1986) too, in his book-length study of the case, focuses to a certain degree upon Ernst's alleged latent homosexuality, again taking the rat torture as the coordinates for this interpretation. Different to Kassabian and Kazanjian (2005), however, Mahoney does not trace his account of homosexuality back to Ernst's early episode of biting. Mahoney instead situates the beginning of the rat obsession with the story told by the cruel captain, "a father figure toward whom the Rat Man had repressed homosexual fantasies" (p. 52). Mahoney does not substantiate why he believes that Ernst had homosexual fantasies about the cruel captain, though he links the fantasy to a dual active and passive orientation on the part of Ernst, desiring to both anally penetrate, and be penetrated by, his father. Later Mahoney suggests that Ernst identified with his mother, who Mahoney depicts as both passively submitting to the father, but also as an intimidating mother (this emphasis upon an intimidating mother is one also made by Künstlicher, 1998). Whilst in general I enjoy Mahoney's extensive examinations of some of Freud's cases, in this particular interpretation of Freud's "Notes upon a case of obsessional neurosis" I cannot affirm what seems to be a rather over-determined account of homosexuality.

Mahoney's claim that Ernst identified with his mother is echoed in the work of Oliver (2011), who suggests that Ernst preferred a feminine position and hence was like his mother. As we know, the "feminine position" referred to by Oliver is nothing like either of the feminine positions within Lacan's formula of sexuation, and instead is based on the assumption that women are normatively feminine and passive, and men are normatively masculine and active. Oliver, for example, infers that Ernst preferred a feminine position on the basis of Freud's suggestion that for Ernst rats were associated with children. Oliver suggests that the rat obsession signifies Ernst's desire to have children, and hence his feminine identification. What a complex set of pink herrings! Oliver seems to presume that anyone who wishes to have children must be feminine, that the mother herself had a feminine identification, and that Ernst followed suit. None of these claims, I would suggest, are logically correct, and instead represent the imposition of a normative reading of what men and women are "supposed" to be upon the case materials.

Returning to Mahoney (1986), he too emphasises the claim that Ersnt displayed a feminine identification. He bases this claim on two aspects of the case. First, we learn in the case that Ernst had an undescended testicle. Mahoney suggests from this that Ernst wondered if his mother too had something hidden within her, and hence identified with her. Turning to the syntax of Ernst's speech, Mahoney (1996) suggests that Ernst's way of speaking—which alternated between rapid pronunciation and mumbling or speaking slowly—was a particularly feminine mode of speech that "disrupted contiguity, created gaps and symbolic anuses to be penetrated, or phobically closed up such gaps" (p. 109). Whilst there is certainly something to be made of Mahoney's claim about the syntax of Ernst's speech (as I do in my analysis below), it is a normative claim to suggest that if in his speech he opened up or closed gaps, this meant he had a feminine identification.

Turning to a Lacanian reading of the case, and following Lacan's (1979) own account of the case in "The neurotic's individual myth", Leader (2003) emphasises a different set of coordinates within the case, ones somewhat more closely align with my own focus below. Rather than focusing on the rat torture, both Lacan and Leader instead emphasis the "absurd scenario" (Leader, p. 40) reported by Freud in which Ernst went to great lengths to repay someone for a set of glasses that they had received delivery of on his behalf. I won't attempt to summarise this scenario here as I will not be exploring it in my analysis below, but suffice to say, what Lacan and Leader make of it pertains to the role of the father's past debts in Ernst's psychic life. The issues of debt, wealth, and dependency raised by Leader are ones that I now explore in my own analysis of the case.

A focus on sexuation

As I noted above, I do not take my coordinates for analysing the case from the account of the rat torture, though as we shall see below, rats nonetheless figure in my interpretation. Instead, I take as my coordinates the relationship between money, marriage, and sex, all of which are repeated themes in the case, and are amplified in the original case notes. The place to start with in terms of unpacking these relationships, I would suggest, is with the mother and father. In establishing the background to the case, Freud tells us that:

> [Ernst's] mother was brought up in a wealthy family with which she was distantly connected. This family carried on a large industrial concern. His father, at the time of his marriage, had been taken into the business, and had thus by his marriage made himself a fairly comfortable position. The patient had learnt from some chaff exchanged between his parents (whose marriage was an extremely happy one) that his father, some time before making his mother's acquaintance, had made advances to a pretty but penniless girl of humble birth. (p. 195)

Whilst an arranged marriage of sorts would have been relatively common at the time, what is most notable about the marriage—and which orients the entire case and indeed, I would argue, Ernst's sexuation—is the fact that his father married into money. What his father was presented with, it would appear, was the option between marrying for money, or marrying for love—what we might think of as a version of Lacan's "your money or your life". The father chose the former, it would appear (though we must acknowledge, as does Freud, that the marriage turned out to be a happy one). In my reading, what is salient about this background to the case is not, however, the choice between money and love. Rather, what I see as particularly salient is what was in effect the *payment for love*. In other words, my central conjecture in this chapter is that Ernst viewed his father as akin to a prostitute—as having been paid to marry and love his mother. As we might expect, the dilemma of money or love, and being paid to love, later repeats for Ernst, as Freud goes on to tell us:

> After his father's death the patient's mother told him one day that she had been discussing his future with her rich relations, and that one of her cousins had declared himself ready to let him marry one of his daughters when his education was completed; a business connection with the firm would offer him a brilliant opening in his profession. This family plan stirred up in him a conflict as to whether he should remain faithful to the lady he loved in spite of her poverty, or whether he should follow in his father's footsteps and marry the lovely, rich, and well-connected girl who had been assigned to him. (p. 199)

Ultimately, as we learn, and unlike his father, Ernst chose to marry for love rather than money, despite vocal opposition from his mother. Nonetheless, the demand that Ernst faced was to follow his father and prostitute himself to marriage. More evidence is provided in the case about the opposition between love and money, specifically in the family narrative I outlined briefly above in regards to the work of Kassabian and Kazanjian (2005), in which Ernst was punished by his father for biting someone:

> When he was very small [...] he had done something naughty, for which his father had given him a beating. The little boy had flown into a terrible rage and had hurled abuse at his father even while he was under his blows. But as he knew no bad language, he had

called him all the names of common objects that he could think of, and had screamed: "You lamp! You towel! You plate!" and so on. His father, shaken by such an outburst of elemental fury, had stopped beating him, and had declared: "The child will be either a great man or a great criminal!" The patient believed that the scene made a permanent impression upon himself as well as upon his father. His father, he said, never beat him again. (p. 205)

There are two key things that interest me in this anecdote, one which pertains to the love or money choice, and another which gives us some idea about how Ernst deciphered the position of his father. In regards to the former, his father's statement that "The child will either be a great man or a great criminal" is one that suggests to me the choice that Ernst faced in terms of love or money. He could marry for love, potentially forsaking wealth, and be a great man, or he could marry for money and in so doing prostitute himself, and by the laws of the time, be a criminal. From an early age, then, Ernst was faced with this choice between greatness and criminality.

The second point that I take from this anecdote pertains to the position of the father. Whilst much has been made previously of Ernst's fear of his father and the sense that his father was a powerful man, here the young rageful Ernst could come up with no better names with which to abuse his father than everyday household objects: "You lamp! You towel! You plate!" There are many other words that Ernst no doubt had at his disposal, words that would have more clearly signified a view of his father as powerful and someone to be scared of. Instead, the words he uses reduce his father to a commonplace, as an item that can be substituted one for another. This, then, was not a person who was the exception, nor was there anything about him that suggested access to any form of jouissance other than the phallic. This, then, was a father in the position of the for-all.

To return to my points above about love or money, Freud provides some further clarification about the anecdote involving Ernst doing something naughty:

> The patient subsequently questioned his mother again [about the episode]. She confirmed the story, adding that at the time he had been between three and four years old and that he had been given the punishment because he had *bitten* some one. She could

remember no further details, except for a very uncertain idea
that the person the little boy had hurt might have been his nurse.
(p. 206)

So here we have a first instance of a rat who bites, in association with
the declaration: "The child will either be a great man or a great criminal." It is possible for us to gain some further clarity about these two
positions from the many associations that Freud reports in the case
between rats, money, and sex (and hence prostitution). Freud tells us
that Ernst shared the expression "So many rats, so many florins" to
describe a range of differing experiences, including paying Freud for
his services. As Freud notes, this expression "could serve as an excellent characterisation of a certain female profession which he particularly detested" (p. 214). For Ernst, then, there was an apparent fear of
being the criminal prostitute who, like is father, is bitten (i.e., has sex)
for money. Instead it would seem, at least at this juncture, that Ernst
desired to be the one who paid to bite someone. This is evident in two
particular associations reported by Freud in the original case notes:

> He had another association, however, to the effect that he need not
> marry his cousin if she only offered herself to him without mar-
> riage, and against this, in turn, the objection that if so he would
> have to pay for every copulation in florins as with the prostitute.
> Thus he came back to his delirium of "so many florins, so many
> rats": i.e., "so many florins, so many tails" (copulations). (p. 313)
>   Another time [in an association] he saw my daughter with two
> patches of dung in the place of eyes. This means that he has not
> fallen in love with her eyes, but with her money. Emmy [the cousin
> his mother wanted him to marry] has particularly beautiful eyes.
> (p. 282)

In the first association, Ernst is torn again between love and money. If
he marries his cousin as his parents wished, then he would be marrying for money, and hence he would be the prostitute who is bitten for
money. On the other hand, if he had sex with his cousin without being
married to her then it would be like having sex with a prostitute, which
would require him to pay her. The second association extends the first
by suggesting that Ernst's vision of Anna Freud with dung in place of
her eyes meant that if he were to marry her, it would be for money, and

hence he would be a prostitute. By contrast, the cousin he was intended to marry had beautiful eyes, yet by marrying her he would by default be marrying for money. Moving beyond these two apparent options, and moving beyond my suggestion above that Ernst wished to be the one paid to bite, I would suggest that Ernst wanted the liberty to have sex with women to whom he was not married, but for whom he would not need to pay. We shall return to this point a little later when we consider Ernst's own sexuated position.

Before turning to Ernst's position, it is useful for us to first consider how he deciphered his mother's position. Two dreams described by Freud in the original case notes provide us with coordinates about the mother:

> [His beloved] lady was under some kind of restraint. He took his two Japanese swords and set her free. Clutching them, he hurried to the place where he suspected she was. He knew that they meant "marriage" and "copulation". Both things now came true. He found her leaning up against a wall, with thumbscrews fastened to her. The dream seemed to him now to become ambiguous. Either he set her free from this situation by means of his two swords, "marriage" and "copulation": or the other idea was that it was only on account of them that she had got into this situation. (p. 267)
>
> My mother's body naked. Two swords sticking into her breast from the side (like a decoration, he said later—following the Lucrece *motif*). The lower part of her body and especially her genitals had been entirely eaten up by me and the children. (p. 282)

Whilst these are reported to us as two separate dreams, it is important, as Freud himself notes, to understand them as connected, given the fact that in the first dream the lady is freed by two swords, and in the second dream the mother has two swords sticking out of her. In terms of the swords, as Ernst tells Freud, the swords represent marriage and copulation. This suggests to me something further about why Ernst struggled with the dilemma of love or money. As I noted above, by marrying for money, his father was in a sense akin to a prostitute. This means, in turn, that his mother was the one who obtained the services of a prostitute. Yet as the dream suggests, it wasn't entirely clear for Ernst whether the swords of marriage and copulation were a liberty for his mother or whether they were the very causes of her restraint. I would suggest that in fact the former was true for his mother, but the latter was true for his father. Let's consider each in turn now.

In terms of the mother, she had grown up in an adoptive family, a wealthy family to whom her birth parents were distantly connected. We are given no further details about his mother's upbringing, but I would conjecture that for her, the marriage freed her from a family life that was like a set of thumbscrews. This sense of marriage as freedom was true even though the marriage led to copulation, which led to the birth of children who then ate up "the lower part of her body and especially her genitals". This was then a person who, despite the apparent ambiguity attached to marriage for Ernst, was someone who desired and indeed enjoyed marriage, copulation, and children. It is not too much of a stretch, I would suggest, to propose that this is a person in the position of the no-exception. Whilst Ernst could not quite identify what it was that propelled his mother to make the choices she made, she was nonetheless propelled by a desire, a desire that potentially represented something of an other jouissance.

The father, on the other hand, only got into the situation he was in on account of marriage and copulation. What precisely this situation was is relayed to us via another dream:

> His father had come back [from the dead]. He was not surprised at this. He was immensely pleased. His mother said reproachfully, "Friedrich, why is it such a long time since we've heard from you?" He thought that they would have to cut down expenses after all, as there would be an extra person living in the house now. This thought was in revenge against his father who, he had been told, was in despair over his birth, as he was over each new baby. (p. 298)

The father was a man, then, who had no choice but to despair over the birth of each child, wondering how he could afford yet another mouth to feed. As I noted above, this was not a person who was all-powerful, and hence could control how many children he had. Instead, this was a person—the for-all—who was in many ways caught in the thrall of the non-symbolisable desire of the no-exception.

Having now established the positions of the mother and father as deciphered by Ernst, we can now turn to consider Ernst's own position. As I have noted throughout my analysis of the case, Ernst's position was a complex one, torn between the injunctions to have love or money. My conclusion is that, as the little rat who bit his nursery maid (and who also, we learn in the case, exhibited other rat-like behaviours), Ernst chose something of a middle ground. He was not going to be the prostitute like his father, the one who was paid money for love. Nor, however, was he going to be the one who paid money for love, as was the case with his mother. Whilst it would seem apparent that his mother's desire was of interest to him (as we shall discuss further below in terms of his fantasy and object *a*), Ernst ultimately was a person who chose love *without* money. We see this in terms of the fact that he ultimately married the lady whom he loved, who came to him without money (and moreover came to him having had her ovaries removed, and hence unable to conceive children with him).

My suggestion, then, is that Ernst chose the position of the not-all: within the terms of his family where phallic jouissance was determined by love or money, but where love required money and money required love, he chose a different route, one where he could have love even if it didn't come with money. Thus counter to Lacan's suggestion that the threat "your money or your life" produces an impossible choice between a life without money or no life at all, Ernst chose the former. In so doing, he chose a sexuated position in which he had access to a specific form of other jouissance, one that involved love freed from the constraints of money.

The question left to explore, then, is the fantasy through which Ernst gained access to his object *a*. Here is where we must take most seriously the figure of the rat for Ernst. Different to the emphasis on the rat as a symbol of sexual intercourse (and anal penetration specifically), my suggestion is that for Ernst he both wanted to be the not-all who could have love without having to worry about the constraints of money, yet at the same time he needed to keep the relationship between sex, money, and marriage in play given that was the currency of his first and second Other's desire as he deciphered them to be. Perhaps most importantly with regard to his mother, is the suggestion by Freud within the original case notes that at an early age a cousin had told Ernst that all women were whores, alongside the fact that as a child Ernst enjoyed playing with his mother's hair whilst it was tied back, referring to it as a rat's tail. In these two, apparently conflicting, accounts of his mother, Ernst, it could be suggested, saw her as both the prostitute who was paid for sex, and the rat who paid for sex. This, I would argue, is emblematic of the elusive position of the mother, one that Ernst sought to capture through a fantasy in which he was a rat who could cross boundaries: he could play at being the one who paid, he could play at being the one who was paid, all the while ensuring that the elusive position of his mother remained accessible, hence overcoming in fantasy the fact of the sexual non-relationship.

Within this fantasy of being the rat who can "creep" about the place and thus dart into the spaces where his mother's elusive desire might reside, we can follow Mahoney's (1996) to suggest that Ernst's object *a* resided within the very syntax of the fantasy itself. In other words, rather than being represented by a specific image or thing that allowed him to feel a sense of oneness with his mother, Ernst's object *a* was a form of language that allowed him to embody the rat who could open up or close down spaces where his mother's desire might reside. Perhaps equally importantly, and again like the rat, in his speech Ernst could hide his fantasy and the object *a* within it in plain sight. He could speak to his mother and others in a form that constantly evoked his fantasy.

Importantly, and to touch once again on the rat torture, we might conjecture that the reason why this was so distressing for Ernst is because it provided a literalisation of his fantasy. This was a torture involving a rat literally creeping around, literally crossing boundaries, and in the end, we are told, both the rat and the prisoner die (the rat from suffocation inside the anus, and the prisoner from being mutilated by the rat). If the fantasy I outlined above is close to true, then its literalisation would indeed be distressing. Not simply, following Lacan, because anxiety occurs when a fantasy is too closely approximated, but moreover because the reality of the fantasy would involve his own death as well as his mother's.

Conclusions

In writing this chapter I was reminded of one of my favourite movies—*Breakfast at Tiffany's*—in which Audrey Hepburn's character Holly Golightly speaks about the men who pay her for "trips to the powder room", referring to them as "rats" and "super rats". This, of course, is a flip of the logic presented above, in which the one who pays is the rat, rather the one who is paid (as I suggested was the case for Ernst). Nonetheless, what it signifies to me is the rat motif as one centrally involving commerce related to sex. And regardless of the position of the rat in each example, this position is always one that is to a degree ambiguous. As Holly tells us, a lover whom she thought to be a "super rat" turned out to be just a scared little mouse, just as the meaning of Ernst's mother's role as a potential rat is always obscured to him. The rat fantasy as I described it above, then, is one that is reliant upon indeterminacy: it resists one simple meaning, and instead is reliant upon the possibility of multiple avenues being open to the rat.

Further in regards to this consideration of the rat fantasy, we must return to the declaration that Ernst would be "either a great man or a great criminal". It would be far too simple to say that in refusing to marry for money, Ernst was a great man. Instead, we might suggest that Ernst refused the terms set by his father. In locating himself within a fantasy that allowed him access to a sense of oneness with his mother, and given his father's position as the for-all who could be substituted for a lamp, a plate or a table, it is not at all surprising that Ernst appears to have rejected the terms set for him by his father. This again serves as a reminder that what is at stake in any examination of sexuation is not the union of a pair, but rather how the sexual non-relation functions, how it is apparent to a child as they enter into language, and how they attempt to negotiate ways that allow them, at least in fantasy, to claim a sense of oneness.

CHAPTER SEVEN

Psycho-analytic notes on an autobiographical account of a case of paranoia

The case

As has been true for many of the other cases I have analysed in this book, to a certain degree Freud's (1911c) "Psycho-analytic note on an autobiographical account of a case of paranoia" provides us with a relatively limited amount of information about the life of the person he subjects to analysis, specifically with reference to his family. Furthermore, and similar in a way to the analysis that Freud provides in his an "Analysis of a phobia in a five-year-old boy", his "Psycho-analytic note on an autobiographical account of a case of paranoia" is also limited by the fact that he did not work personally with the person he subjects to analysis. Instead, his analysis is based on the personal memoirs of Daniel Paul Schreber, a German judge who was twice hospitalised due to psychosis. Yet despite this relative lack of information about Schreber's family, the second-hand nature of the information available (provided by Schreber himself), and the complex nature of the information available in the memoirs (which primarily focuses on the extensive and complex delusions that Schreber experienced), in this chapter I will argue that there is nonetheless something useful to be made of the information available to us. Indeed Lacan, in his seminar on *The Psychoses*, shared a similar view:

> Chapter three of the *Memoirs*, in which he gave reasons for his neuropathy and developed the notion of soul murder, was censored. Still, we know that it contained remarks concerning his family, which would probably have thrown light both on his initial delusion in relation to his father and brother, or to someone else close to him, and on what are commonly called the significant transferential elements. But that censorship is not as regrettable as all that, ultimately. Sometimes too many details prevent the basic formal features from being seen. What is essential is not that, because of the censorship, we should have lost the occasion to understand such and such an affective experience concerning those close to him, but that he, the subject, failed to understand it and yet was able to formulate it. (1997, p. 76)

Importantly, and given the widespread view that Schreber did indeed display a psychotic structure, in this chapter my analytic focus is not *per se* on identifying sexuated positions. Such positions, as I outlined in chapter two, are the product of both an individual's attempts via fantasy to maintain a sense of oneness with their first Other (through the belief that the individual can be what it is that the first Other desires), and the "no" of the second Other which serves to regulate the overwhelming jouissance that would come from having unmitigated access to the first Other. In the case of a psychotic structure, the "no" of the second Other (or something or someone that represents it) has failed or is faulty, and hence the individual experiences themselves as in a perpetual state of oneness with their first Other, and hence as overwhelmed by jouissance. Their own sexuated position is thus to a certain degree moot, and the positions of their first and second Other as deciphered by them are also to a degree moot.

Nonetheless, and again following Lacan (1997), there is considerable utility in examining why the "no" of the second Other failed (or was faulty), and stemming from this what we might glean about the individual's understanding of their first Other, seen as one to whom the individual with a psychotic structure believes they have unmitigated access. Whilst these two positions (of first and second Other)—along with the indications of the position of the individual who displays a psychotic structure—do not neatly map across to Lacan's formula of sexuation in ways that allow for a simple interpretation (in contrast to the other cases analysed in this book, where this was to a degree possible), focusing on the sexuated coordinates apparent in psychosis may nonetheless be useful.

Given the fact, as I indicated above, that the materials available to us in Freud's discussion of Schreber's memoirs are somewhat limited (and are circumscribed by Freud's particular interpretation of them, as we shall see shortly), it is necessary for me in this chapter to go beyond Freud's discussion of the case. Specifically, I draw upon historical accounts of Schreber's life, the memoirs written by Schreber, and a poem written by Schreber after he had left the institutions in which he stayed during his second bout of psychosis. These materials, I suggest, give us some insight into the failure of the "no" of Schreber's father and the position of his mother as a consequence.

Before moving on to examine previous accounts of the case, it is important to note Freud's particular focus within his analysis of the case. Unlike in other chapters, I will not attempt to summarise his account in any great detail, largely because his account is premised upon Schreber's memoirs (which are highly complex, and which to a certain degree resist a simplistic summary and which are only minimally my focus below). What we can usefully summarise about Freud's account is his emphasis upon latent homosexuality as a cause of psychosis. As we shall see in regards to many of the previous Freudian accounts of the case, this equation of homosexuality with psychosis is an ongoing theme in post-Freudian literature, one that constitutes a significant pink herring in the Freudian oeuvre, and one that has potentially been the most harmful.

Specifically in regards to Freud's account, he suggests that Schreber experienced a latent homosexual desire for his father (and possibly his older brother), and that when he began to have dreams about a possible relapse into psychosis, these were driven by this homosexual desire, which had been displaced from the father (or brother) onto the clinician who had treated his first psychosis—a Professor Flechsig. The fact that a significant proportion of Schreber's delusions centred upon Flechsig, Freud suggests, demonstrates that Schreber's unconscious longing for Flechsig brought on his second psychosis. For Freud, latent homosexual desire is thus both a cause of psychosis, and subsequently shapes the delusions themselves (which, Freud suggests, were a response to the relative disinterest shown by Flechsig towards Schreber during his second psychosis).

An equally concerning pink herring apparent in Freud's reading of the case is his equation of Schreber's delusion of "turning into a woman" with his supposed desire for a passive homosexual relationship with Flechsig. This specific focus upon a presumed relationship between psychosis and a delusion of "turning into a woman" has, since Freud, been translated by some writers into a case for a relationship between psychosis and identifying as transgender. As I will discuss in the following section, whilst differential diagnosis is of course always important, the spectre of psychosis continues to haunt clinical responses to transgender people.

Previous accounts

Following the approach I adopted in summarising previous accounts of Freud's "Fragment of an analysis of a case of hysteria", in this section I first examine accounts that appear to be (or which position themselves) as Freudian, and then go on to examine those that are explicitly Lacanian. As we shall see, and bearing in mind the points I made above in terms of Freud's interpretation of the case, the distinction between these two sets of accounts is important.

Given my summary of Freud's interpretation above, it is perhaps understandable that those who have adopted a Freudian account of the case have emphasised homosexuality. Of those who have emphasised homosexuality, Rosenbaum (2005), Alanen (2009), and White (1961) are perhaps the clearest examples. For Rosenbaum, homosexuality is seen as a step along the pathway to a normative heterosexuality. In the case of psychosis, however, Rosenbaum goes beyond Freud's emphasis upon homosexuality as unconscious in the case of psychosis, to instead emphasise that psychoses occur as a result of an inability on the part of homosexual individuals to form a link with a "group of like-minded others" (p. 84). It appears that Rosenbaum is suggesting that psychosis occurs when someone who displays a homosexual orientation is unable to make a wider connection with a community of people who are also homosexual. This lack of connection, Rosenbaum suggests, is both a product of psychotic structure, and the cause of psychosis. In my reading, this is not only a pink herring (the correlation of homosexuality to psychosis), but also something of a chicken or egg argument, in that

Rosenbaum appears to shift between treating a psychotic structure as preventing connection to a homosexual community, and treating a homosexual orientation as a precursor to a desire for connection. How psychosis (as opposed to a simpler claim such as social isolation preventing the formation of links with others) mediates these claims is unclear in Rosenbaum's account.

Also adopting a Freudian approach, and with specific reference to Schreber, Alanen (2009) identifies "repressed homosexual feeling" towards Flechsig (p. 25) as the cause of Schreber's second psychosis, and White (1961) suggests that Schreber's delusion of turning into a woman was a "homosexual fantasy" (p. 60). White's account is largely illogical, in that if we are to believe that Schreber desired to become a woman, then his feelings for Flechsig were not homosexual at all, but indeed would be heterosexual. As we shall see below, however, treating Schreber's delusion as evidence of a transgender identity is misguided.

Another writer who has adopted a Freudian approach to the case is Lothane (1989; 1993), whose historical work has provided an important corrective to the work of authors such as Niederland (1974), the latter of whom has narrated a particular interpretation of the historical materials related to Schreber that serves to construct Schreber's father as a tyrant, and who has suggested that most of Schreber's delusions can be traced to abuse by the father. Lothane corrects this particular reading through his own analysis of the historical materials, and his work is particularly convincing in this regard. Nonetheless, Lothane's own interpretation of Schreber's delusions is subject to its own limitations, specifically in regards to the delusion of turning into a woman.

In discussing Lothane's (1989; 1993) account, it is important to note that he does indeed distinguish between delusion and reality. In other words, Lothane acknowledges that the delusion of turning into a woman was indeed a delusion, and not the expression of a transgender identity. Nonetheless, Lothane's account is limited to a degree by the ways in which he accounts for Schreber's delusion. Specifically, he reduces the delusion of turning into a woman to "a metaphor for being controlled and helpless" (1989, p. 238), as a form of "reparation of the loss [of a child carried by Schreber's wife] by the fantasy [...] of being able to bring forth children" (1993, p. 134), and as a form of feminine identification with his mother. These claims about Schreber's delusion of turning into a woman are, as I will demonstrate in my analysis below, a misreading of the broader structures in which the delusions existed, reliant as Lothane's account is upon the delusion as a form of maternal emulation, rather than as a form of positioning in relation to maternal jouissance.

Moving to Lacanian accounts of the case, we can more clearly see how a focus on positioning rather than emulation is useful. Most importantly, Lacanian accounts of the Schreber case have suggested that the issue at stake is related to the position of The Woman in the mathemes that accompany Lacan's formula of sexuation. As I elaborated in chapter two, due to the fact that, unlike the masculine side of the equation, the feminine side of the equation does not rely upon an exception, the feminine side of the equation is an open set. From this, Lacan derives his claim that there is no The Woman. By this he does not mean that there are no women or that women are not speakingbeings. Rather, he means that on the feminine side of the equation there is no essence of an other jouissance. Instead, those located on the feminine side of the formula are both entirely subject to the phallic function, but at the same time have access to an other jouissance that is not phallic.

In terms of a psychotic structure, and following Lacan, writers such as Ragland (2004), Gherovici (2010), and Wilden (1972) have suggested that in terms of positioning, an individual who has a psychotic structure believes they can choose the position of The Woman. In regards to Schreber, Ragland, for example, suggests that he "went as far as becoming God's wife to retain his primary identification with his own mother as The Woman who exists" (p. 26). Gherovici expands upon this, by suggesting that:

> Schreber's imposed feminisation was a way to write the jouissance of the Other. Jouissance was equated with a signifier, "the" woman, who was placed in the position of Other. Schreber was to become "the" woman that was needed to grant the jouissance of the Other [...] [This served to stabilise the] psychosis, supporting jouissance while securing a sexual rapport that does not exist. (pp. 177–178)

The final point from Gherovici is important, as it signals that whilst Schreber's delusion of turning into a woman was indeed a delusion premised upon the unconscious belief that he could occupy the position of The Woman, it was nonetheless one driven by the desire to overcome, in fantasy, the sexual non-relationship. In this sense, it is of a kind with the modes of fantasy analysed in previous chapters, which hence provides a logic for why, in my analysis below, I cautiously examine the sexuated positions as they appear in materials related to Schreber's life. Gherovici's work further demonstrates the merits of this approach:

> In Lacan's sexuation formulas, the symbolic phallus requires the correlate of a barred Woman. If the name of the father is foreclosed, the Woman exists as a delusional substitute, equivalent to the exception of the primal father. The Woman functions as an ideal image of the body as an empty envelope that produces jouissance, a jouissance beyond the phallus, the jouissance of the Other [...] Lacan wrote that, because Schreber was "unable to be the phallus the mother is missing, there remained the solution of being the woman that men are missing". (p. 180)

Despite being a product of the failure of the "no" of the father, and despite being formed in the context of a delusion, Schreber's fantasy (that he could occupy the position of The Woman) allowed him access to an other jouissance that had its correlates in the position of the exception on the masculine side. This is a point I will take up in my own analysis of the materials.

Albeit in slightly different language, Wilden (1972) also takes up this point about Schreber being in the position of The Woman, where he suggests that:

> To be a Woman, for Schreber, does not mean to exchange one set of genitals for another. To be a Woman means to be totally in touch with the source of human life. TO BE THE WOMAN MEANS IN FACT NOTHING LESS THAN TO BE A HUMAN BEING. (p. 299, capitals in original)

Echoing Lothane's (1989; 1993) point above, Wilden is clear that the delusion of turning into a woman does not signify a transgender identity. Instead, and similar to Gherovici (2010), Wilden suggests that being The Woman allows Schreber to claim a place of totality: of having complete access to both phallic and an other jouissance. Perhaps lacking from Wilden's account is a discussion of the fact that this belief in being able to occupy both positions (and thus overcome the sexual non-relationship) is impossible, though his work nonetheless signifies the key issue at stake in the delusion as I suggested above, namely one of positioning, rather than identification. We can now turn to examine this more closely with regard to a small selection of materials related to Schreber's life.

A focus on sexuation

In order to cautiously examine what might be ascertained about the positions of Schreber's father and mother, I now draw on materials from Lothane's (1989; 1993) historical analysis of the relationship between Schreber and his father, in addition to discussions by Israëls (1988) and de Oliveira (1988) in regards to a poem written by Schreber (1988) on the occasion of his mother's ninetieth birthday.

In terms of the father, Lothane (1989; 1993) refutes Niederland's (1974) claim that Schreber was abused by his father. The father, as has been widely reported, was well known for his development of parental techniques that aimed to promote healthy, moral living, including physical exercise and restraint from masturbation. His books feature diagrams of apparatus that could be used to encourage children to, for example, sit properly whilst eating, and lie properly whilst sleeping. Niederland suggests that these apparatus were applied to Schreber by his father, and that the memories of these abuses (specifically being bound across the chest to the point of having his breathing restricted) were what repeated in the delusions.

Lothane (1989; 1993) argues instead, that in the years during which Schreber's father was most active in his work (prior to an illness that led to his death), Schreber was outside the age range in which the father advocated for the use of the various apparatus. Instead, Lothane suggests that, from the age of ten, Schreber's father was largely bedridden, and far too unwell to be subjecting Schreber or his siblings to abuse. At the same time, however, Lothane does acknowledge that regardless of whether or not abuse occurred, "Schreber's father was idealised as a social reformer during his son's and Freud's lifetime and for many decades thereafter" (1989, p. 215).

As Lacan argues, contrary to Freud, the "no" of the father may fail not because the actual father as second Other is too weak, but rather because he is too strong. This may be a father who *makes* laws (in a formal sense), rather than being seen by the child as someone who is also subject to the law. Schreber's father, it would seem, was both an inadequate parental figure in many ways (with his focus on work more

than on his children, and subsequently with his illness preventing him
from spending time with his children), yet the broader narrative about
him was of a great man, one who arbitrated over how children should
be treated, and hence potentially beyond the purview of the law. Due to
this prevarication between the two positions, I hesitate to apportion a
particular position to Schreber's father. Indeed, given the operations of
a psychotic structure, it suffices to say that the "no" of Schreber's father
failed or was faulty, and thus Schreber could not accord to him a position that would function to mediate his relationship to his first Other.

Which brings us to Schreber's mother. Whilst to a certain degree
Schreber's father has been given increased attention over the past three
decades in terms of debates about whether or not he was abusive.
Schreber's mother has still remained very much an elusive figure. The
exception to this is the work of White (1961), who provides an extrapolation from information available at the time. Importantly, White's work
is not derived from primary documents, so we must be cautious in
interpreting what he offers. White suggests that Schreber's relationship
to his mother was always mediated by the father, who sought to regulate the mother's child-rearing practices in line with his professional
and moral beliefs. This was a woman, then, who according to White
was in the early part of Schreber's life entirely regulated by the phallic
function. It is tempting to extrapolate to suggest that when his father
became bed-ridden when Schreber was aged ten, the mother came out
from under the shadow of the father, thus undermining the authority
of the father and presenting herself as a powerful figure of authority.
Such an account, however, is simplistic, is not necessarily supported
by historical evidence, and ignores the fact that a psychotic structure
is typically formed well before a child is ten (i.e., it is typically formed
at the point where the child's entrance into language is marked by a
failure of the "no" of the father).

With this in mind, what then can we make of Schreber's mother?
I take as incisive a comment made by Lacan in his discussion of the
case, where he suggest that "what characterises Schreber's world is that
this *he* is lost, and only the *you* remains" (Lacan, 1997, p. 101). If this
"you" is the mother unbounded, the mother as unregulated jouissance,
then what evidence might we find to support this claim? The evidence
for this claim comes primarily from the aforementioned poem written
by Schreber for his mother, but also from his memoirs. In his memoirs,
Schreber (2000) makes a number of references to Goethe and his work.

Two particular instances are of note. The first pertains to a discussion provided by Schreber in regards to souls. Souls, he suggests, ascend to heaven after death, and there they may, for a potentially limited period of time, retain the memory of their life on earth. In heaven, suggests Schreber, souls can receive information about loved ones still on earth, but this is not upsetting because souls in heaven do not have very good memories (hence if they learn of something negative about a loved one on earth, they are soon to forget it). Despite the ability to remember their earthly memories (but not remember for long any new information they receive once in heaven), Schreber suggests that soon enough souls lose all memories of their time on earth. This, however, does not apply to all people, suggest Schreber. Certain exceptional souls such as Goethe, claims Schreber, retain their memories for centuries.

The second key reference to Goethe in Schreber's (2000) memoirs is when he introduces the concept of "soul-murder". Whilst, as Lacan (1997) notes, much of the information about soul-murders contained in the original manuscript of the memoirs was declared unfit to print (and hence was redacted), Schreber does tell us that the idea of soul-murder "is widespread in folklore and poetry of all peoples [...] [an idea which involves the belief that] it is somehow possible to take possession of another person's soul in order to prolong ones' life at another soul's expense, or to secure some other advantages which outlast death" (p. 33). As an example of these types of folklore, Schreber cites, amongst others, the work of Goethe (and in particular, his *Faust*).

How, then, does this relate to Schreber's mother? The reason why I have chosen to focus on the apparently central role of Goethe in some of Schreber's memoir is due to the poem he wrote on the occasion of his mother's ninetieth birthday. The poem narrates his mother's life, from the time of her birth until the time of her ninetieth birthday. Many parts of the poem could be subject to analysis (given it is the only writing by Schreber on the topic of his mother that is available), however my interest is in the final part of the poem. Two "riddles" are presented at the end of the poem. The first—which is my focus here—can be deciphered as referring to the word "fireball". As Israëls (1988) notes, Fireball (or Feuerkugel in German) is the name of the house in which Schreber's mother was born. Importantly, in the opening stanzas of the poem we are told that as a child the mother had been shown the windows of a room in the house next door where Goethe had lived as a student. Years later, when the Goethe Society wanted to commemorate this location, the mother was the one who could answer as to which windows.

So here we have a riddle written for the mother, referring to her birth and her intimate, indeed unique, relationship to Goethe (i.e., she was the only one who could identify his windows), a man whom in his memoirs Schreber refers to as an example of an exceptional soul who could retain his memories after death for many centuries, and who, Schreber presumes, knew enough about soul-murders to write about them. This was a man, in Schreber's estimation, who not only knew, but who could remember, and who could learn about things that happened on earth after his death and remember them (as opposed to other souls, who would forget). Might we suggest, then, that Schreber's mother, through her unique relationship to Goethe, was someone who might be remembered, at least in Schreber's eyes? Indeed, and given the mother's advanced age, might she not be someone who could somehow have taken the soul of another (i.e., Goethe's) and thus have cheated death?

These, of course, are considerable extrapolations, and we must be very cautious about them. Nonetheless, my suggestion here is that in lieu of the proper functioning of the "no" of the father, and despite White's (1961) claim that Schreber's mother was under the spell of the father, we might suggest that Schreber saw his mother as a powerful being, as one who was above death, above the law of the father, and thus as something akin to God. If so, following Gherovici (2010), we might suggest that Schreber saw his mother in the position of the exception.

Having presented this possibility, I would follow Gherovici (2010) and Wilden (1972) in suggesting that Schreber believed himself to be in the position of The Woman: as the wife of God. Importantly, and as I discussed above, we are not talking here about a desire to become a woman in the physical sense. As I have repeated throughout this book, our focus on sexuation is not on assigned sex. Rather, our focus is on positions with Lacan's formula of sexuation. Of course The Woman is excluded in Lacan's formula—her non-existence is the reason why the feminine side of the equation is an open set. Yet for Schreber, with a psychotic structure, these same rules do not apply. Nonetheless, and as I hope I have demonstrated in my analysis above, this does not mean that there are no rules. Instead, the rules are a fantasy based on the overwhelming jouissance of the mother, who is experienced as being one with Schreber. That he would see them as paired in a union—as having foreclosed any recognition of the sexual non-relationship— would suggest that it is logical that Schreber would inhabit a fantasy in which he is the wife of God: the partner of his mother. And this is precisely what we see in the memoirs. Despite Freud's focus on Flechsig (and without wishing to undermine the very real possibility that Flechsig was indeed a tyrant to Schreber, his patient), perhaps Flechsig is a pink herring. Perhaps the elaborate delusional system that centres the rays of God as they shine down on Schreber and transform him into a woman, perhaps the notion that he might be fucked by God, is in fact Schreber's account of his sense of overwhelming oneness with a mother who was not prohibited to him due to the failure of the "no" of the father, and who was associated for Schreber, it would seem, with a powerful figure such as Goethe.

Conclusions

The Lacanian reading I have offered of selected portions of materials related to Schreber's life, I would suggest, offers us something of considerable value in terms of the overall message of this book. By putting aside Freud's pink herrings in relation to latent homosexuality, and putting aside the equation of the delusion of turning into a woman with a transgender identity, an alternate, Lacanian, reading of the case highlights why it is so vitally important to understand that sexuation is of an entirely different register to assigned sex and those to whom one is attracted. Whilst it might be surprising that the case of Schreber is the place where this has become most evident, it is the place precisely because we are working with coordinates that don't neatly align with Lacan's formula of sexuation. This, however, does not undermine the importance of having worked with the formula in other chapters. Instead, and as Lacan argued through his seminar on *The Psychoses*, a psychotic structure has much to tell us about why the entrance into language can fail, and thus why even when it "succeeds", it is only barely scraping over the line. Indeed, as Lacan (1997) suggests:

> *Verdichtung* [condensation, for Freud, and thus metaphor, for Lacan]
> is simply the law of misunderstanding, owing to which we survive
> or, even, owing to which we can, if we are a man, for example, completely satisfy our opposite tendencies by occupying our feminine

position in a symbolic relations, while perfectly well remaining a
man equipped with one's virility on both the imaginary and the
real planes. (p. 83)

That this law of misunderstanding is true for all speakingbeings perhaps explains why it would be the rule for people who display a psychotic structure. Importantly, this claim, based on a focus on sexuation,
is not in any way a claim about latent homosexuality or transgender
identification. Rather, my claim is that it is completely understandable
that a failure of the "no" of the father would result in an individual
with a psychotic structure creating their own signifiers for sexual difference, and thus their own unique account of the relationship between
individuals in terms of the masculine and feminine. What this suggests
to me is that those with a psychotic structure are not wholly outside the
formula of sexuation nor social understandings of what it means to be
a man or a woman, heterosexual or homosexual, but rather negotiate
their own ways of making sense of these signifiers that as Lacan suggested, refer to signifieds that are undifferentiated. If anything, cases
such as Schreber's highlight for us the sexual non-relationship in all its
glory, a point I will return to in the following, final, chapter of this book.

CHAPTER EIGHT

A clinic of sexuation

As I have emphasised throughout this book, in focusing on sexuation my intention has not been to make a claim that certain sexuated positions "naturally" coalesce in relation to one another. Indeed, such a claim would be entirely antithetical to the argument that I have presented in this book, given the fact that the sexuated positions that we may decipher from an analysis are themselves reflective of the decipherings of the analysand with regard to their first and second Other. In other words, there is no universal truth to be derived from a focus on sexuation in regards to how particular positions relate to one another. Instead, what we are working with are the operations of fantasy in which positions are deciphered on the basis of a desire to achieve a sense of oneness and thus overcome the sexual non-relationship. The important point to remember, then, is that what I have offered in my analysis of each case is an interpretation of each analysand's fantasy, but from which I have not sought to claim that there are consistent patterns of sexuation that can then be directly mapped across onto other cases.

Despite these caveats, however, it is useful here to summarise the positions identified in each case, and to place these alongside the diagnoses of structure (neurosis, perversion, and psychosis) made by Freud, and also alongside Freud's commentaries about identification and object choice. My reason for doing this is not *per se* to make the case that the patterns identified through my analyses will hold out with regard to other cases, but instead to demonstrate what can be gained from a focus on sexuation. These summaries provide a background from which, in the remainder of this chapter, I then explore some key aspects of what a clinic of sexuation might involve.

Recapitulations

In order to summarise the cases, in this section I use a series of tables that provide two sets of comparisons, the first being between my account of sexuated positions and a Freudian account of structure, and the second being between my account of fantasy and object *a* and a Freudian account of identification and object choice. As we shall see, there are gaps in all of the tables, which are a product of the lack of information we have about most of the parents in terms of a Freudian account of structure. I would also note that I have chosen not to include a table on Freud's "Psycho-analytic note on an autobiographical account of a case of paranoia", given this was a case of psychosis and hence my analysis in the previous chapter only provided a very tentative account of the case in terms of sexuation.

In summarising the five cases in tabular form, I follow each with a brief comment in terms of general trends that might suggest to us something about how sexuation operates in relation to structure and symptomology.

"The psychogenesis of a case of homosexuality in a woman"

	Sexuation	Freudian structure
Mother	No exception	
Father	Exception	
Sidonie	For-all	
The Lady	No exception	

	Sexuation		Freudian Interpretation
Fantasy	Giving a child	**Identification**	Masculine
Object *a*		**Object Choice**	Feminine

This first case, alongside the following case, is interesting for a number of reasons. Both of these cases indicate a constellation of sexuated positions that differ from the other three cases summarised here (which display the same set of positions with regard to the analysand, mother, and father). Again, my point here is not to suggest that there *should* be similarities across cases. Instead, my interest here is the context in which the differences exist. In this first case, the analysand did not present to Freud with symptoms, and was not given a formal diagnosis of structure. In the following case, the diagnosis of structure has been debated, whilst in the remaining three cases a diagnosis of neurosis was clearly warranted. Whether or not the similarity between these latter three cases in terms of sexuation bears any relationship to their similarity in terms of structure bears further investigation in the future.

"From the history of an infantile neurosis"

	Sexuation	Freudian Structure
Mother	For-all	
Father	For-all	
Sergei	Equivocation	Phobic/Obsessional
Sister	Exception	

Sexuation		Freudian Interpretation	
Fantasy Is had and has		**Identification** Feminine	
Object *a* Wings as equivocation		**Object Choice** Feminine and Masculine	

As I argued in my analysis of this case, and different to "The psychogenesis of a case of homosexuality in a woman" (which involved an asymptomatic analysand), Sergei's complex positioning as an equivocation between the exception and the for-all is potentially a product of the deciphering of his parents via the position of his sister, who I interpreted as being located in the position of the exception. This perhaps explains why the positions are quite different to those in the cases below, in addition to the fact, as Abraham and Torok (1986) suggest, that Sergei may have had a perverse, rather than neurotic, structure.

"Fragment of an analysis of a case of hysteria"

	Sexuation	Freudian Structure
Mother	No exception	Obsessional
Father	For-all	
Dora	Not-all	Hysteric
Frau K.	No exception	
Herr K.	For-All	

	Sexuation		Freudian Interpretation
Fantasy	Death of father and brother	**Identification**	Masculine
Object *a*	Being what remains	**Object Choice**	Feminine

Freud's "Fragment of an analysis of a case of hysteria" is the first of three cases that present the same set of sexuated positions with regard to the analysand, the mother, and the father. Of course these positions are located within the context of entirely different fantasies, so comparisons must be undertaken cautiously. Nonetheless, there is some utility in noting these similarities, especially when compared to the previous two cases, one of which involved an asymptomic analysand, and the second of which potentially involved an analysand who displayed a perverse structure. In other words, the first two cases summarised above may potentially be different because they *don't* report on neurotic analysands, whereas these other three cases do.

"Analysis of a phobia in a five-year-old boy"

	Sexuation	Freudian Structure
Mother	No exception	
Father	For-all	
Hans	Not-all	Phobic

	Sexuation		Freudian Interpretation
Fantasy	To have a child	**Identification**	Masculine
Object *a*	Mother's ambivalence	**Object Choice**	Feminine

Of note with regard to Freud's "Analysis of a phobia in a five-year-old boy" is the fact that this is the only case where identification and object choice, in Freudian terms, appear to be normatively related (i.e., heterosexual). Of course all of the caveats applied in my analysis of the case must also be applied here: Freud himself did not directly undertake the analysis (but rather the father did); we don't know anything from the case materials about how Hans identified later in life; and we must take serious the contention that in many ways this wasn't necessarily an analysis, but rather a series of conversations between a child and his father, the latter of which was invested in generating analytic materials.

"Notes upon a case of obsessional neurosis"

	Sexuation	Freudian Structure
Mother	No exception	
Father	For-all	
Ernst	Not-all	Obsessional

	Sexuation		Freudian Interpretation
Fantasy	Crossing Boundaries	**Identification**	Feminine
Object *a*	Openings	**Object Choice**	Masculine

To reiterate: my aim in presenting tabular summaries of the five cases has not been to make any grand claims about sexuation that could then be simplistically applied to other cases. Nonetheless, I do find it interesting that there are similarities in sexuation across the three cases that may be most clearly labelled as involving a neurosis. That the other two cases do not adhere to this pattern, I suggested above, may be because they did not involve a neurosis. Given my emphasis in this book upon the formula of sexuation as a mode of accounting for how, in fantasy, we attempt to negotiate the sexual non-relationship, these differences are thus of interest. This is a point I will take up in more detail in the following section.

Family relations

The different ways in which people attempt to negotiate a fantasy that would seek to overcome the sexual non-relationship (and hence provide them with access to a sense of oneness) is potentially a useful avenue for future practice and research. Such an avenue would allow us to ask questions such as: "How do the deciphered positions of an individual's first and second Other potentially play out in other relationships later in life?" With regard to Lacan's formula of sexuation (which focuses on positions, rather than identifications), our approach to answering this type of question would likely be less focused on "solutions" (i.e., deciphering sexuation so as to provide an answer to a symptom), and more about mapping out how certain positions repeat.

As such, when interpreting the sexuation of an individual analysand within the context of their immediate family, whilst we must be cautious in inferring any type of truth about the relationship between the position of their first and second Other (i.e., by suggesting that two particular sexuated positions "naturally" go together), we can nonetheless consider how certain modes of jouissance coalesce and how this speaks both to an individual's claim in fantasy to overcoming the sexual non-relationship, in addition to how certain modes of jouissance seek their fulfilment in fantasies that are shaped by the relationships between particular sexuated positions.

In my own practice, some of these ideas inform how I engage in work with families. Whilst obviously family therapy is an entirely different modality to psychoanalysis, there are interplays between the two that can be harnessed. For example, in some instances I have worked both with individuals in the form of an analysis, but have also worked separately with them and their immediate family members. This dual approach has been driven by a belief both that there are family-level symptoms, and that there are individual symptoms, and that the two are separate but interrelated. To a certain degree Billig (1999) makes this case in his book *Freudian Repression*, in which he argues for a reinterpretation of some of Freud's cases though the lens of rhetorical analysis. Billig suggests that the dynamics within the cases, which Freud attributed to the unconscious, may more correctly be attributed to the interactional styles of the family members. Whilst I do not agree with Billig's suggestion that the unconscious can be reduced to interpersonal conversational processes, I nonetheless see considerable merit in his suggestion that within family dynamics we can see the operations of particular modes of being.

My approach in this book, however, has not *per se* been focused on rhetoric, but rather on fantasy and sexuation. Nonetheless, as I indicated above, there is something to be made of the idea that we can work at multiple levels (i.e., individual and familial), and that a focus on sexuation can help to bring these two levels together by identifying how the individual in analysis deciphered the positions of their first and second Other, how they then chose to locate themselves, and how these positions have implications for how the analysand navigates adult life. A focus on sexuation in this context allows us to both further the analysis through identifying fantasy and its role in mitigating the sexual non-relationship, and how this may specifically play out in familial dynamics. Importantly, my suggestion here is not that we would utilise family therapy to verify the sexuated positions identified in an analysis. Such recourse to the "truth" of a family would add nothing to the analysis. Instead, my suggestion is that knowledge produced by the analysand in one context might fruitfully be harnessed to contribute to therapeutic work being undertaken in another (i.e., familial) context.

Freud's own position and the transference

In addition to using the insights produced by a focus upon sexuation within an analysis to inform therapeutic work in a familial context, we can also harness the focus upon sexuation to achieve other outcomes. A key example of this, which I discussed in a number of chapters in this book, pertains to the transference. In Freud's "The psychogenesis of a case of homosexuality in a woman" in particular, it would appear that the analysand sought to refuse Freud a position that would allow him to approximate the position of both her mother and her beloved Lady.

There has, of course, been much discussion about the transference with regards to Freud's cases, particularly with regard to both "The psychogenesis of a case of homosexuality in a woman" (see chapters in Lesser & Schoenberg , 1999) and "Fragment of an analysis of a case of hysteria" (see chapters in Bernheimer & Kahane, 1985). Such discussion has typically emphasised how Freud potentially mishandled the transference, specifically by offering constructions that spoke too openly of the analysand's fantasy. I certainly would not dispute such suggestions, but nonetheless would seek to extend them by considering how a focus on sexuation might additionally help us to understand the operations of the transference.

It is commonplace to acknowledge that "not every analyst suits every analysand". People bring with them a range of stereotypes and preferences, both conscious and unconscious, that shape how they view a potential analyst. Many of these, of course, can be overcome in the course of the analysis. Some, however, may stubbornly refuse interpretation, instead presenting a barrier to the progress of the analysis. My suggestion here is not, of course, that we should focus on sexuation early on in an analysis so as to identify any potential barriers that might inhibit progress. Rather, my suggestion is that a focus on sexuation may help us to understand instances where the transference does not function, or where it functions in ways that seem to inhibit the analysis. This would not mean that the analyst would attempt to appear in a position that is more amenable to the analysand—this type of performance is only likely to result in problems for the analysis. Instead, my proposal is that we develop ways to harness issues related to sexuation that arise in an analysis.

Harnessing instances, such as in Freud's "The psychogenesis of a case of homosexuality in a woman", where an analysand resists the analyst (potentially as a result of how they have deciphered their sexuated position), is no guarantee that the analysis will proceed, but it does offer us another way to think about working with the transference. Specifically, a focus on sexuation may offer a way of presenting constructions that bring to the fore the particular dynamics that may be preventing the analysand from making headway with their symptom. It is one thing to note when an analysand displays resistance that appears to be the product of the transference, and another thing altogether to offer a construction that may help them to work through that resistance. A focus on sexuation and positions within a fantasy with regard to the analyst may offer one concrete way in which to work with resistances arising from the transference.

The politics of sexuation

In my analysis of Freud's "Fragment of an analysis of a case of hysteria", I suggested that a focus on sexuation is not inherently apolitical. This is a point worthy of further discussion here. Importantly, my claim that there is a politics attached to sexuation is not intended to suggest *per se* that our readings of sexuation should be politically motivated. It would be unfortunate, for example, to see readings of sexuation that make unwarranted claims about an analysand simply to make a political point. Any consideration of sexuation should always be based upon the analytic material and should be capable of incorporating, at its broadest, the discourse of the unconscious as elaborated by the analysand. In other words, any claims about sexuation should attempt to make the most comprehensive interpretation of the analytic material, rather than providing a reductive account so as simply to make a political point.

With this clarification in mind, what we can say about the politics of a focus on sexuation pertains primarily to questions of agency. As was the case in Freud's "Fragment of an analysis of a case of hysteria", my particular interpretation of Dora's positioning and fantasy allowed me to emphasise her agency in the events that occurred in her life. I did this not to naively transpose her unconscious fantasy onto her everyday life: my aim was not to suggest *per se* that Dora's position as the not-all inherently disposed her to resistance to social norms. Rather, my point was that her choice of position was an agentic choice, albeit one prescribed by a desire in fantasy to foster a sense of oneness with her first Other.

Of course, as I outlined in the introduction to this book, on the one hand, the choice of sexuation isn't really much of a choice at all, given the other option is to not enter into language and to remain at one with the mother and hence be overwhelmed by her jouissance and thus potentially experience psychosis. In this sense, there might not appear to be a whole lot of agency in the choice of sexuation. At the same time, however, there is a sense in which the way that one chooses to position oneself demonstrates how unconscious positions within a structure are not predetermined: they are not produced through a direct relationship between the "fact" of the first and second Other's positions. Instead, each person negotiates their own way to resist the fact of the sexual non-relationship.

This understanding of the politics of sexuation, then, provides a radically different account of children than might be the case in a standard developmental account. The latter, at its broadest, sees children as programmed to follow a particular normative pathway, which thus serves to minimise children's own desires and agency. Whilst when speaking about sexuation we are speaking at the level of the unconscious, we are nonetheless acknowledging that, as speakingbeings, most children take an active role in their own positioning, and in so doing are not simply the (by)products of their parents. As I noted above, this is not to say that familial dynamics have nothing to do with an individual's position: Rather, they have everything to do with it. But this is not the same as saying that children are passive recipients of their parents' ministrations. Instead children, both consciously and unconsciously, make agentic choices about the ways in which they will position themselves, even if such agency is bound by the fact of the sexual non-relationship and the castrating effects of the entrance into language and the "no" of the father.

The politics of sexuation, as I understand, is thus a politics of choice within constraint, which is a fairly accurate reflection of the world in which we live. Furthermore, such an understanding of psychoanalysis more broadly resists the interpretation of analytic practice as deterministic and constraining. Instead, as I have suggested here, an analysis in which an individual can speak about the operations of their fantasy, their position within it, and the broader frameworks that both constrain and make their fantasy possible, is an analysis that holds a liberatory potential. Liberation, not in the sense of freedom from one's position, but rather freedom in the sense of knowing how one is positioned, and the choice that led to that position.

What of (homo)sexuality?

As we come to the end of this book, it is salient to return to the questions that to a certain degree shaped my own analysis, and specifically my question about why I am gay. At certain points in writing this book I have felt this question slip further and further to the wayside. This, of course, has been necessary, given my contention that a focus on homosexuality constitutes something of a pink herring. Nonetheless, there is still some utility in considering what a focus on sexuation has to tell us about sexual orientation.

Perhaps at its simplest, what I believe this book tells us about homosexuality is that the fact of the sexual non-relationship and the position that one chooses in terms of sexuation are of an entirely different register to one's experience of one's sexual orientation. In a slightly different fashion, Lacan too makes this point:

> Now, is the activity/passivity relation identical with the sexual
> relation? I would ask you to refer to a passage in the Wolf-Man, for
> example [...]. There Freud explains in short that the polar reference
> activity/passivity is there in order to name, to cover, to metaphorise
> that which remains unfathomable in sexual difference. Nowhere

does he ever say that, psychologically, the masculine/feminine relation is apprehensible otherwise than by the representative of the activity/passivity opposition. As such, the masculine/feminine opposition is never attained. (Lacan, *Seminar XI*, 1977, p. 192)

I take Lacan as suggesting here that the binary of active/passive attempts to write a truth about the sexual non-relationship: it attempts to convert what is impossible (i.e., sexual rapport) into a possibility, by seeing relationships as configured by the association between what are treated as matched pairs. In other words, whilst in the unconscious there is no sign for sexual difference, in everyday life we act as though there can be a truth about sexual difference.

With regard to homosexuality, then, whilst the word "homosexuality" itself rests upon the idea of sameness (i.e., "homo"), common-sense understandings of the lives of lesbians and gay men rely upon the assumption that within a lesbian or gay couple there will be difference, and that this difference represents the fact of sexual difference. So, for example, lesbian or gay couples may be asked "Which one's the woman?", or "Who is the top and who is the bottom?" These types of questions represent an attempt at marking sexual difference. Of course a common response to these type of questions is to insist that homosexual relationships do not mirror heterosexual relationships: that there does not need to be someone in an active position and someone in a passive position, or someone in a masculine position and someone in a feminine position. This type of response, however, only allows for a very narrow understanding of homosexuality in terms of sexuation. Instead, I would suggest the importance of acknowledging difference on altogether different register.

Another common assumption made, particularly about gay men, is that we are attracted to *all* men. This is an assumption typically made by heterosexual men, who presume that all gay men wish to have sex with them. This type of assumption ignores the fact that whilst gay men are attracted to other men, we, like all speakingbeings, are attracted to something about a potential partner in terms of the object *a*. Thus whilst homosexuality might at first glance appear to fall to the wayside in my account of sexuation, in fact a focus upon sexuation gives us an entirely different way to think about desire amongst people who identify as lesbian or gay. It allows us to resist the imposition of normative binaries, but also to resist the injunction to respond to such binaries by stating that lesbians and gay men are governed by our own set of rules. Whilst socially this may be very much true, at the level of the unconscious this type of claim is something of a pink herring, as it accepts the premise that there is something fundamentally different about lesbian and gay desire in terms of sexuation.

Of course it is important to clarify that I am not dismissing the unique ways in which lesbians and gay men often configure our relationships in the context of a heteronormative society. These modes of relationality, however, are to a certain degree matters for a different type of analysis than one that focuses upon sexuation. At the same time, a focus upon sexuation with regards to lesbians and gay men would not be entirely separate, in the context of therapeutic work, from an investigation of the effects of social norms. It will always be important for clinicians to acknowledge the broader circumstances shaping an individual's current experiences, and for many lesbians and gay men this unfortunately often continues to include experiences of discrimination. And of course when working within the register of sexuation we are working with fantasy, and fantasy is what shapes the types of relationships we engage in and the people we feel attracted to. In this sense, a focus on sexuation is central to understanding the relationships that lesbians and gay men enter into, though this is no more true than is the case for any other population group comprised of speakingbeings.

Conclusions

As I noted in the introduction to this book, my writing sits in a context of a diverse range of literatures that contribute to our understanding of psychoanalysis. Particularly with regard to other writers who take up Lacan's formula of sexuation (e.g., Barnard, 2002; Gherovici, 2010; Morel, 2000; Ragland, 2004; Soler, 2006), my hope is that this book has made a useful contribution to how we might apply an understanding of sexuation to clinical cases. Given this book is limited by its focus on existing case materials provided by Freud, it will be important that into the future the framework that I have outlined in this book is applied to contemporary cases. Only then will the true merits and scope of the framework I have offered become apparent.

The diverse communities of people collectively known as "transgender" constitute one particular group of people with whom I think the framework I have outlined in this book could productively be applied. As I noted in the previous chapter, clinical responses to transgender people have often been limited in the context of psychoanalysis by the unhelpful association between psychosis and a transgender identity. In this book, I have argued that this association is both flawed and pathologising. Given the nature of the cases I was working with in this book, I was unable to explore the relevance of a focus upon sexuation to the lives of transgender people (though see Gherovici, 2010, for an engagement with this topic). My hope is that into the future there will be opportunities to productively engage with the framework I have outlined in this book and its possible utility for transgender people.

Given the fact of the sexual non-relationship, it is perhaps unsurprising that there is an endless proliferation of cultural texts that attempt to overwrite this fact with a claim to the truth of sexual difference, and hence the possibility of the sexual relationship. From romance novels to Valentine's Day cards, from dating websites to the focus upon "attachment parenting", in so many ways we see attempts at writing a truth about sexual difference. Yet despite all of these phenomena, the sexual non-relationship is something which we must all, in our unconscious, come to grapple with. This, to me, suggest why, despite the steady stream of new modalities aimed at bringing people happiness or relief from a symptom, psychoanalysis continues to enjoy at place at the table of therapeutic approaches.

Psychoanalysis, I believe, has enjoyed continued interest because it affords us ways to make do. It helps us to understand that a liveable life requires us to make peace with how we came to be who we are. Focusing on sexuation, I have suggested, provides another avenue through which to engage in this process of making peace. Whilst this might sound pessimistic or as engendering a sense of futility, instead I would suggest that getting by in life despite the fact of the sexual non-relationship is actually a significant achievement. Different to a psychological focus on self-actualisation, however, psychoanalysis allows us to understand the cost of becoming a speakingbeing, how loss and gain are one and the same thing, and that knowing oneself is always a fraught process that brings with it the requirement to accept alienation not only from others, but from our selves.

REFERENCES

Abelove, H. (1993). Freud, male homosexuality, and the Americans. In: H. Abelove, M. A. Barale, & D. Halperin (Eds.) *The Lesbian and Gay Studies Reader* (pp. 381–393). New York: Routledge.

Abraham, N., & Torok, M. (1986). *The Wolf Man's Magic Word: A Cryptonymy*. Minneapolis: University of Minnesota Press.

Adams, P. (1996). *The Emptiness of the Image: Psychoanalysis and Sexual Differences*. Oxon: Routledge.

Alanen, Y. O. (2009). The Schreber case and Freud's double-edged influence on the psychoanalytic approach to psychosis. In: Y. O. Alanen, M. González de Chávez, A -L. S. Silver & B. Martindale (Eds.), *Psychotherapeutic Approaches to Schizophrenic Psychoses* (pp. 23–37). New York: Routledge.

Barnard, S. (2002). Tongues of angels: Feminine structure and other jouissance. In: S. Barnard & B. Fink (Eds.), *Reading Seminar XX: Lacan's Major Work on Love, Knowledge and Feminine Sexuality* (pp. 171–186). Albany: State University of New York Press.

Bernheimer, C., & Kahane, C. (Eds.) (1985). *In Dora's Case: Freud-Hysteria-Feminism*. New York: Columbia University Press.

Bersani, L. (1995). *Homos*. London: Harvard University Press.

Bersani, L. (2009). *Is the Rectum a Grave? And Other Essays.* Chicago: Chicago University Press. Billig, M. (1999). *Freudian Repression: Conversation Creating the Unconscious.* Cambridge: Cambridge University Press.

Butler, J. (1992). The lesbian phallus and the morphological imaginary. *Differences, 4*: 133–171.

Butler, J. (2002). *Antigone's Claim: Kinship Between Life and Death.* Columbia University Press.

Connell, R. W. (2000). *The Men and the Boys.* Sydney: Allen & Unwin.

Corbett, K. (2009). Little Hans: Masculinity foretold. *The Psychoanalytic Quarterly, 78:* 733–764.

Davis, W. (1995). *Drawing the Dream of the Wolves: Homosexuality, Interpretation, and Freud's "Wolf Man".* Indianapolis: Indiana University Press.

Dean, T. (2000). *Beyond Sexuality.* Chicago: Chicago University Press.

Dean, T., & Lane, C. (Eds.) (2001). *Homosexuality and Psychoanalysis.* Chicago: University of Chicago Press.

de Lauretis, T. (1994). *The Practice of Love: Lesbian Sexuality and Perverse Desire.* Indianapolis: Indiana University Press.

de Oliveira, P. (1988). Schreber, ladies and gentlemen. In: D. B. Alison, P. de Oliveira, M. S. Roberts & A. S. Weiss (Eds.), *Psychosis and Sexuality: Toward a Post-Analystic View of the Schreber Case* (pp. 169–179). Albany: State University of New York Press.

Domenici, T., & Lesser, R. C. (Eds.) (1995). *Disorienting Sexuality: Psychoanalytic Reappraisals of Sexual Identities.* New York: Routledge.

Drescher, J. (1998). *Psychoanalytic Therapy and the Gay Man.* New York: Routledge.

Edelman, L. (1991). Seeing things: Representation, the scene of surveillance, and the spectacle of gay male sex. In: D. Fuss (Ed.) *Inside/Out: Lesbian Theories, Gay Theories* (pp. 93–116). New York: Routledge.

Ferraro, D. (2010). Feminine positions and the wolf man. Available at: www.lacancircle.net/wp-content/uploads/2012/01/Ferraro-Feminine-Positions-and-the-Wolf-Man.pdf

Fink, B. (1991). There's no such thing as a sexual relationship: Existence and the formulas of sexuation. *Newsletter of the Freudian Field, 1(2):* 59–85.

Freud, S. (1905e). Fragment of an analysis of a case of hysteria. In: *The Standard Edition of the Complete Psychological Works of Sigmund Freud, Vol VII.* J. Strachey (Trans.). London: Vintage.

Freud, S. (1909b). Analysis of a phobia in a five-year-old boy. In: *The Standard Edition of the Complete Psychological Works of Sigmund Freud, Vol X.* J. Strachey (Trans.). London: Vintage.

Freud, S. (1909d). Notes upon a case of obsessional neurosis. In: *The Standard Edition of the Complete Psychological Works of Sigmund Freud, Vol X.* J. Strachey (Trans.). London: Vintage.

Freud, S. (1911c). Psycho-analytic notes on an autobiographical account of a case of paranoia (dementia paranoides). In: *The Standard Edition of the Complete Psychological Works of Sigmund Freud, Vol XII*. J. Strachey (Trans.). London: Vintage.

Freud, S. (1910h). A special type of choice of object made by men. *The Standard Edition of the Complete Psychological Works of Sigmund Freud, Vol XI*. J. Strachey (Trans.). London: Vintage.

Freud, S. (1918b). From the history of an infantile neurosis. In: *The Standard Edition of the Complete Psychological Works of Sigmund Freud, Vol XVII*. J. Strachey (Trans.). London: Vintage.

Freud, S. (1920a). The psychogenesis of a case of female homosexuality. In: *The Standard Edition of the Complete Psychological Works of Sigmund Freud, Vol XVIII*. J. Strachey (Trans.). London: Vintage.

Freud, S. (1937b). Moses an Egyptian. In: *The Standard Edition of the Complete Psychological Works of Sigmund Freud, Vol XXIII*. J. Strachey (Trans.). London: Vintage.

Fuss, D. (1993). Freud's fallen women: Identification, desire, and "A case of homosexuality in a woman". *Yale Journal of Criticism, 6*: 1–23.

Gallop, J. (1985). Keys to Dora. In: C. Bernheimer & C. Kahane (Eds.) *In Dora's Case: Freud-Hysteria-Feminism* (pp. 200–220). New York: Columbia University Press.

Gherovici, P. (2010). *Please Select Your Gender: From the Invention of Hysteria to the Democratizing of Transgenderism*. New York: Routledge.

Goodwin, T. W. (2012). Freud, the Wolf Man and the encrypted dynamism of revolutionary history. *European Journal of Psychoanalysis*.

Hamer, D. (1990). Significant others: Lesbianism and psychoanalytic theory. *Feminist Review, 34*: 134–151.

Hertz, N. (1985). Dora's secrets, Freud's techniques. In: C. Bernheimer & C. Kahane (Eds.), *In Dora's Case: Freud-Hysteria-Feminism* (pp. 221–242). New York: Columbia University Press.

Israëls, H. (1988). Introduction to the new Schreber texts. In: D. B. Alison, P. de Oliveira, M. S. Roberts & A. S. Weiss (Eds.), *Psychosis and Sexuality: Toward a Post-Analytic View of the Schreber Case* (pp. 204–215). Albany: State University of New York Press.

Jacobus, M. (1995). Russian tactics. Freud's "Case of homosexuality in a woman". *GLQ, 2*: 65–79.

Kassabian, A., & Kazanjian, D. (2005). From somewhere else. *Third Text, 19*: 125–144.

Künstlicher, R. (1998). Horror at pleasure of his own of which he himself is not aware: The Case of the Rat Man. In I. Matthis & I. Szecsödy (Eds.), *On Freud's Couch: Seven New Interpretations of Freud's Case Histories* (pp. 127–162). New Jersey: Aronson.

Larcano, E. (2005). A "pink" herring: The prospect of polygamy following the legalization of same-sex marriage. *Connecticut Law Review, 38*: 1065–1111.

Layton, L. (1999). *Who's that Girl? Who's that Boy? Clinical Practice Meets Postmodern Gender Theory*. London: Jason Aronson Inc.

Lacan, J. (1977). *The Seminar of Jacques Lacan, Book XI*. J. -A. Miller (Ed.), A. Sheridan (Trans.). New York: W.W. Norton and Company.

Lacan, J. (1979). The neurotic's individual myth. *The psychoanalytic quarterly, 48*: 405.

Lacan, J. (1997). *The Psychoses 1955–1956. The Seminar of Jacques Lacan, Book III*. J. -A. Miller (Ed.), R. Grigg (Trans.). New York: Norton.

Lacan, J. (1998). *On Feminine Sexuality: The Limits of Love and Knowledge 1972–1973. Encore: The Seminar of Jacques Lacan, Book XX*. J. -A. Miller (Ed.), B. Fink (Trans.). New York: Norton.

Lacan, J. (2007). *Écrits*. B. Fink (Trans.). New York: W.W. Norton & Company.

Lacan, J. (2014). *Anxiety*. J. -A. Miller (Ed.), A. R. Price (Trans.). Cambridge: Polity.

Laplanche, J., & Pontalis, J. (1986). Fantasy and the origins of sexuality. In: V. Burgin, J. Donald & C. Kaplan (Eds.), *Formations of Fantasy* (pp. 5–34). New York: Routledge.

Leader, D. (2000). Beating fantasies and sexuality. In: R. Selecl (Ed.), *Sexuation* (pp. 106–130). Durham: Duke University Press.

Leader, D. (2003). Lacan's myths. In: J. -M. Rabaté (Ed.), *The Cambridge Companion to Lacan* (pp. 35–49). Cambridge: Cambridge University Press.

Lefort, R. (1994). *Birth of the Other*. M. Du Ry, L. Watson, & L Rodríguez (Trans.). Chicago: University of Illinois Press.

Le Gaufey, G. (2005). Towards a critical reading of the formulae of sexuation. C. Gallagher (Trans.). *L'unebévue, 22*.

Le Gaufey, G. (2006). *Le Pastout de Lacan: Consistance Logique, Consequences Cliniques*. Trans. C. Gallagher. Paris: Epel.

Lesser, R. C., & Schoenberg, E. (Eds.) (1999). *That Obscure Subject of Desire: Freud's Female Homosexual Revisited*. New York: Routledge.

Lewes, K. (1988). *The Psychoanalytic Theory of Male Homosexuality*. New York: Meridian.

López, A. (2005). The gaze of the white wolf: Psychoanalysis, whiteness, and colonial trauma. In: A. H. López (Ed.), *Postcolonial Whiteness: A Critical Reader on Race and Empire* (pp. 155–181). Albany, NY: State University of New York.

Lothane, Z. (1989). Schreber, Freud, Flechsig, and Weber revisited: An inquiry onto methods of interpretation. *Psychoanalytic Review, 76*: 203–262.

Lothane, Z. (1993). Schreber's feminine identification: Paranoid illness or profound insight? *International Forum of Psychoanalysis, 2*: 131–138.

Mahoney, P. J. (1996). *Freud's Dora: A Psychoanalytic, Historical and Textual Study.* New Haven: Yale University Press.

Mahoney, P. J. (1986). *Freud and the Rat Man.* London: Yale University Press.

Morel, G. (2000). Psychoanalytical anatomy. In: R. Selecl (Ed.), *Sexuation* (pp. 30–37). Durham: Duke University Press.

Morris, C. E. (2002). Pink herring and the fourth persona: J. Edgar Hoover's sex crime panic. *Quarterly Journal of Speech, 88*: 228–244.

Niederland, W. G. (1974). *The Schreber Case: Psychoanalytic Profile of a Paranoid Personality.* New York: Quadrangle.

O'Connor, N., & Ryan, J. (1993). *Wild Desires and Mistaken Identities: Lesbianism and Psychoanalysis.* London: Karnac.

Oliver, K. (2011). Little Hans's little sister. *philoSOPHIA, 1*: 9–28.

Pluth, E. (2007). On sexual difference and sexual "as such": Lacan and the case of Little Hans. *Angelaki: Journal of the Theoretical Humanities, 12*: 69–79.

Ragland, E. (1995). Psychoanalysis and courtly love. *Arthuriana, 5*: 1–20.

Ragland, E. (2000). Lacan and the *homosexuelle*: "A love letter". In: T. Dean & C. Lane (Eds.), *Homosexuality and Psychoanalysis* (pp. 98–119). Chicago: University of Chicago Press.

Ragland, E. (2001). The psychical nature of trauma: Freud's Dora, the Young Homosexual Woman, and the fort! da! paradigm. *Postmodern Culture, 11*.

Ragland, E. (2004). *The Logic of Sexuation.* Albany: State University of New York Press.

Ragland, E. (2006a). Dora and the Name-of-the-Father. *The Symptom.*

Ragland, E. (2006b). The hysteric's truth. In: J. Clemens & R. Grigg (Eds.), *Jacques Lacan and the Other Side of Psychoanalysis* (pp. 69–87). Durham: Duke University Press.Rieder, I., & Voigt, D. (2003). *Sidonie Csillag: Homosexualle chez Freud, Lesbienne dans le Siècle.* Paris: Epel.

Rodríguez, S. A. (1995). The public and the private: The process of sexuation in the boy. *Analysis, 6*: 40–49.

Rose, J. (1985). Dora: Fragment of an analysis. In: C. Bernheimer & C. Kahane (Eds.), *In Dora's Case: Freud-Hysteria-Feminism* (pp. 128–146). New York: Columbia University Press.

Rosenbaum, B. (2005). Psychosis and the structure of homosexuality: Understanding the pathogenesis of schizophrenic states of mind. *The Scandinavian Psychoanalytic Review, 28*: 82–89.

Ross, J. M. (2007). Trauma and abuse in the case of Little Hans: A contemporary perspective. *Journal of the American Psychoanalytic Association, 55*: 779–797.

Roughton, R. (2002). Rethinking homosexuality: What it teaches us about psychoanalysis. *Journal of the American Psychoanalytic Association, 50*: 733–763.

Rudnytsky, P. L. (2000). "Mother, do you have a wiwimaker, too?": Freud's representation of female sexuality in the case of Little Hans. In P. L. Rudnytsky & A. M. Gordon (Eds.), *Psychoanalyses/Feminisms* (pp. 39–53). New York: State University of New York Press.

Schreber, D. P. (1988). Poem for his mother's ninetieth birthday (1905). In: D. B. Alison, P. de Oliveira, M. S. Roberts & A. S. Weiss (Eds.), *Psychosis and Sexuality: Toward a Post-Analytic View of the Schreber Case* (pp. 232–265). Albany: State University of New York Press.

Schreber, D. P. (2000). *Memoirs of my Nervous Illness.* New York: New York Review of Books.

Sherman, E. (2005). *Notes from the Margins: The Gay Analyst's Subjectivity in the Treatment Setting.* New Jersey: The Analytic Press.

Soler, C. (2000). The curse on sex. In: R. Selecl (Ed.), *Sexuation* (pp. 39–56). Durham: Duke University Press.

Soler, C. (2006). What Lacan said about women: A Psychoanalytic Study. J. Holland (Trans.). New York: Other Press.

Swales, S. S. (2012). *Perversion: A Lacanian Psychoanalytic Approach to the Subject.* New York: Routledge.

Van Haute, P., & Geyskens, T. (2012). *A Non-Oedipal Psychoanalysis? A Clinical Anthropology of Hysteria in the Works of Freud and Lacan.* Belgium: Leuven University Press.

Watson, E. (2013). Some considerations of feminine homosexuality. *Lacunae, 2,* 16–28.

White, R. B. (1961). The mother-conflict in Schreber's psychosis. *The International Journal of Psychoanalysis, 42*: 55–73.

Wilden, A. (1972). *System and Structure: Essays in Communication and Exchange.* London: Tavistock Publications.

Žižek, S. (1999). The seven veils of fantasy. In: D. Nobus (Ed.), *Key Concepts of Lacanian Psychoanalysis* (pp. 190–218). New York: Other Press.

Žižek, S. (2002). The real of sexual difference. In: S. Barnard & B. Fink (Eds.), *Reading Seminar XX: Lacan's Major Work on Love, Knowledge and Feminine Sexuality* (pp. 57–76). Albany: State University of New York Press.

Žižek, S. (2005). *Interrogating the Real.* London: Bloomsbury.

INDEX

Abelove, H. xxviii
Abraham, N. 38–39, 42–44, 46–47,
    49, 121
absurd scenario 95
Adams, P. 62–63
Alanen, Y. O. 33–34
anal eroticism 39–40, 43, 93
anal fixation 39
anal intercourse 40–41
angelic femininity 27
"anus" 91
"arse" 91

Barnard, S. 2, 6, 55
"bent-over female," 42
Bernheimer, C. 59–62
Bersani, L. 40
Breakfast at Tiffany's 102
Butler, J. xxix

capacity, to bear child 29
"caress" 89
case studies
    Dora 55–58
    Hans 76–77, 87. *See* Little Hans
    Margarethe Trautenegg 21–23
    Sergei Pankejeff 37–39
clinic of sexuation 119
"coax" 89
"copulation" 99–100
Connell, R. W. 90
conscious reality 52
Corbett, K. 78–80
countertransference 39
"creep" 102
"cryptonomy," 42

Davis, W. 37, 41–43, 49, 51–52
Dean, T. 19

excretory function 43
homosexual and heterosexual
    gratifications 42
matched pair and 40
previous accounts of 39–44
sexuation and 44–52
undifferentiated partners and 41
Israëls, H. 112, 114

Jacobus, M. 24–25
jouissance 8
    access to 10, 16, 30, 32, 34, 48, 50,
        65, 67
    failed 6–7
    identification of 51–52
    loss of 17
    modes of 4, 11
    other 6, 10, 68–69, 72
    Other's desire and 12
    phallic 5–6, 9–10, 66–69

Kahane, C. 50, 59–62
Kassabian, A. 93, 96
Kazanjian, D. 93, 96
Künstlicher, R. 94

Lacan, J. 2–4, 7, 16, 27, 33, 52, 65, 69,
        73, 89, 95, 106, 113–114, 116,
        129
    point 90
    sexuation formulas 111
    suggestion 101
Lacan's formula of sexuation 4–9, 94,
        111, 124
    feminine side 6–8
    masculine side of 5–6
    mother's desire and 13
    mother's feminine sexuation 13
    phallic function (Φ) in 5
    phallic jouissance 5
    representation of 5

lack of desire and authority 78
Lanzer, Ernst 91–92
Laplanche, J. 17
Larcano, E. xviii
Layton, L. xxix
Le Gaufey, G. xxix, 7–8, 11, 15
Leader, D. 70, 95
Lefort, R. xxvii
lesbian desire 26
Lesser, R. C. 21–22, 125
Lewes, K. xxviii
liberation 128
Little Hans 37, 76–90
López, A. 39
Lothane, Z. 109, 111–112

Mahoney, P. J. 56, 62, 64–66, 68, 70,
        93–94, 102
marriage 99
masculine lesbians 26
matched pair 40
maternal emulation 110
Memoirs 106
Morel, G. 130
Morris, C. E. xviii

nationalism 39–40
Niederland, W. G. 109, 112

object a 2–3, 9–15, 28, 51–52
object-cause-of-desire 18
obsessional neurosis 91, 93
obsessive exercise 92
O'Connor, N. xxviii
Oedipus complex 93
Oliver, K. 94
oneness 2

paranoia 105
phallic function (Φ) 5–10, 13, 19–20,
        30–32, 34, 66–68